Lisa,
One of the good things
to come out of the epidemic
is that we became friends!
I enjoy keeping in touch with
you via facebook. Keep smiling!
Love,
Judy

Between Hearts

Judy Humphrey

REBEL
MAGIC

Published by Rebel Magic Books

www.rebelmagicbooks.com

ISBN: 9798416931575

Front cover photograph by Barbara Hudson, 'Snappy Seniors'
Rear cover photographs © Judy Humphrey
Rainbow over Arizona Memorial, Pearl Harbor, Hawaii
Author's backyard in winter
Above the Clouds, taken from helicopter over Napali Coast, Hawaii
Fawns in the Quinnipiac River, author's backyard

To contact the author, visit: www.rebelmagicbooks.com

REBEL
MAGIC

To my son and daughter, Michael and Maureen,
and their father Ed, my first love.
To my grandchildren, Christina, Calvin, Casey, Aiden, and Caira,
and my great grandsons Hayden and Jaxson.
To my second husband Lennie, my greatest love,
who died too young,
and to my stepdaughter Rebecca.
Thank you for being part of my life.

My family July 2019
Back: Caira, Mike, Calvin, Maureen, Casey, Aiden.
Front: Hayden, Judy, Jaxson, Christina.

Contents

1.

The Day I Died

On February 13, 1997, my fiancé Lennie and I took the day off work. We both worked for a state agency. Lennie was having his trigger finger repaired. The surgery went well, and we arrived back home around 10 a.m. I was reading the paper and having my second cup of coffee when I felt a twinge in my left shoulder. It felt like a pinched nerve. It lasted two minutes, then it disappeared.

At lunch time, I felt it again – still a little twinge, but it lasted for five minutes. Lennie suggested I go to the nearby walk-in clinic. He of course came with me but I had to drive because his hand was bandaged. I told the nurse at the desk that I had a pinched nerve in my shoulder. She led me into a treatment room where the doctor did an EKG. That confused me because I couldn't imagine what my heart had to do with my shoulder. The test was normal. I was given a copy and told to return if the pain reoccurred.

When we got back home, I helped Lennie unload a bookcase from his car and set it up in the house. An hour later, the pinch came back stronger. It lasted fifteen minutes. Lennie wanted me to go back to the clinic, but I refused. I figured I'd be sent home again. Besides, the pain stopped.

At 6 p.m., the pain returned much stronger. No matter how I positioned my arm or shoulder, it would not ease up. Pain traveled from my shoulder down my left arm, and my fingers were numb. I didn't know what was happening. Lennie called

911, ignoring my protests. Thank God! Help arrived in under two minutes – a police officer, followed by two paramedics rolling a stretcher. They gave me a tiny tablet to dissolve under my tongue and took my blood pressure.

I wailed, "What's happening? What's wrong with me? I can't feel my fingers – my left hand is numb. Talk to me, somebody, please!"

The medics told me to calm down – I was hyperventilating, causing the numbness in my hand. They sent Lennie, who was hovering over me, to find a paper bag. They told me to take slow, deep breaths into the bag. That didn't help.

By now the pain had overtaken the upper part of my body – it felt like an elephant stepping on my chest. The medics gave me another tablet, with no results. They strapped me in a seated position on the stretcher and wheeled me out to the ambulance. I was terrified. I still didn't know what was going on. Before taking off, one of the medics attempted to start an IV while repeating, "Time is muscle, time is muscle." The longer I was in pain, the more heart muscle I would lose.

The driver asked me, "Where would you like to go?"

"How about Disney World? I haven't been there yet. Where do you usually take people in this condition?"

"To one of the three area hospitals."

"Then take me to the nearest one – the one with the new emergency tower. But I'd rather go to Disney."

I don't remember much of the ride. The medic finally gave up on starting the IV after poking me several times and having me yell at him to "stop fishing in my veins."

The EMTs brought me to a curtained area in the emergency room where three people started working on me, hooking me up to a monitor, getting IVs started, and putting an ID bracelet on my wrist. I was sitting on the bed watching the monitor.

Suddenly, the lines on the monitor began making big up and down trails. I looked over at the tech to my right and said, "I feel funny, like I'm going to faint." As I was passing out, I remember thinking, "Oh, God, I am sorry for every mean, rotten thing I've ever done in my entire life."

The next thing I remember was a feeling that I was floating in space. I opened my eyes, and I was bobbing up near the ceiling watching the activity below. Machines were beeping, lights were flashing, and five people were crowded into the cubicle. The medics flattened the head end of my gurney. Everyone was moving quickly. I realized I had no more pain, no more anxiety, no more fear. Just a feeling of total peace.

"Wow, I guess I just died," I thought. "What a curious feeling." I waved to the figure on the gurney. "Goodbye, me."

2.

Papa and Me — 1946

I called my grandfather Papa because that's what my aunts and uncles called him. My first words were "Papa's hat" and "beer." I remember his hat. It was gray with a wide brim. It hung on a rack by the door and he only wore it during the winter. I used to wait for Papa to get home from work and settle into his red leather chair by the stove, his pipe in one hand, a beer in the other. When he saw me coming, he would set the beer down and let me climb onto his lap. His leather chair made a funny squeak when he moved. His pipe smelled like a wood-burning fire. Papa would pick up his mug and let me drink the foam off the top. My aunt and mother clucked in the background saying he should not give beer to a little kid. That didn't stop him. He'd wait until they weren't looking and sneak me another sip. I didn't particularly like the taste but Papa's sharing it with me made it special.

My grandparents were born in Italy near Avellino, a small town inland from Mt. Vesuvius, south of Naples. My grandmother, Giuditta Maria Russo, came to the US with her family when she was 13 years old. At age 17, my grandfather, Antonio Montella, immigrated with his father. Antonio and Giuditta met for the first time in Waterbury, Connecticut, where both of their families settled. They married in 1898 and lived in Waterbury until Antonio had a disagreement with Giuditta's family. He loaded his family and possessions into a wagon and walked from Waterbury to Bristol, where they spent the rest of their lives.

Antonio Montella, 1876-1949

Giuditta Maria Russo, 1880-1930

I grew up in the family home in Bristol, CT. It had three apartments: two floors and an attic access on the family side, and two smaller apartments on the other side. The family apartment housed my grandfather, Aunt Anna, and a couple of uncles. My parents lived in the second-floor apartment when I was born. The door between our apartment and the family side was never locked. I could visit with my grandfather anytime. Because of this, I have many memories of him even though I was only six years old when he died.

My mother was the eighth of twelve children and the youngest of the four girls. She was seventeen when her mother died. Four cousins were named after our grandmother Giuditta – Judith in English. Giuditta never saw any of her nineteen grandchildren. She died at the age of forty-eight when her youngest son was only 9 years old. The responsibility of the family fell to my Aunt Anna. We called her Zizi Annie, aunt in Italian. She was the oldest. She remained single and took care of everyone, especially Papa. She also died at age 48 in 1950, a year after her father passed away.

I loved the activity in the family home; uncles, aunts and cousins coming and going in the kitchen, the main gathering place. There was always the smell of something wonderful cooking on the stove; most often, tomato sauce with basil. Sunday meals were always communal.

Sometimes, Papa would share a snack with me before dinner. He loved big purple grapes which he ate whole, crunching the seeds. He'd laugh at me when I spit the seeds out. I would perch in his lap so that when he laughed his belly would bounce me up and down. I was a tiny child and he called me his china doll.

One day Papa got sick and went to the hospital. When he came back, he stayed in his bedroom all day. Occasionally, he would come downstairs to eat or sit by the stove. My mother and Zizi Annie were both nurses and they took care of Papa. I heard them say he had cancer and I was told I could not sit in his lap anymore. He rested in his bedroom for a few months but kept getting sicker. No matter how he felt, he always grinned when I popped my head in to see him. Mom and Zizi told me not to bother him. However, he would hold his hand out to me and smile as if we shared a secret.

Early one morning, Dad woke me up and said that my sister and I had to stay with my Irish grandmother in New Britain for a few days. I knew something was wrong because we'd never done that before. When Mom brought a suitcase to the car with our clothes in it, her eyes were all red from crying. It was still dark out and we were in our pajamas. We slept at Grammy's house for three nights and when we got back home, Papa was gone. His red leather chair sat beside the stove for a few months after he died. When no one was looking I'd climb in it to see if I could make it squeak like Papa did.

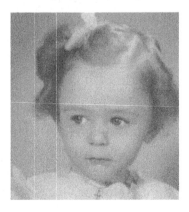

Papa's china doll

3.

Daddy, Grammy, and Dad

Daddy ran away from home when he was 15. He was a self-taught musician who played saxophone and clarinet. He joined a band of musicians in the Borscht Belt, an area of predominantly Jewish resort hotels that catered to wealthy guests in the Catskill Mountains of New York.

Nightly entertainment featured vaudeville acts – singers, jugglers, magicians, comedians and acrobats. They were accompanied by music. Dance bands flourished in the 1930s. Daddy played with the Dorsey brothers, Tommy and Jimmy, and Benny Goodman's bands.

I didn't know anything about Daddy's youth until I had kids of my own. I guess he thought by then we were old enough so he told my sister and me some of his escapades He'd tell ghost stories to the girls who hung out with the band to convince them the hotel was haunted. The group of musicians who bunked together got in deep trouble one summer and almost lost their housing. It had started with a few drops of water and ended with an all-out battle with garden hoses – indoors.

My dad worked in the Catskills seven months each year and then return to New Britain and go back to high school. The last time he returned home, a boy he'd begun high school with was now one of his teachers. Daddy was in his 60s when he finally received his high school diploma. He earned the credits he needed through an adult education program by playing clarinet in the town symphony orchestra.

The oldest of three boys, John Kenneth Humphrey, got off to a shaky start. He was born underweight, weak and sickly. Grammy told me that to keep him warm, she would place him in a blanket-lined roasting pan. Then she'd turn the oven on low, open the door, and set the pan on it. Back then, houses weren't heated well.

Grammy, Kathryn Agnes (Dunn) Humphrey, had a lifelong devotion to the Infant of Prague. I didn't come upon the reason for her devotion until I travelled to Prague in the Czech Republic. When I visited the statue of the Infant, in the Church of Our Lady Victorious, I discovered that the Infant is the patron of children and health. Grammy kept the statue in her home and dutifully changed the garments according to the Church seasons. Grandchildren were not allowed to play with the Infant.

What I remember most about my grandmother is her pies. She made the best apple pie with flaky golden-brown crust that melted in your mouth. She taught me her pie-making secrets while I was still in grade school. The biggest tip is that the surface you're working on, and the utensils, have to be cold. Use only ice water in the recipe and do not handle the dough. I've passed her secrets along to my granddaughters and to my stepdaughter. I don't think Grammy would mind.

Grammy talked loudly – she was totally deaf in one ear – and clanged pots and rattled dishes while cooking. She had a boisterous laugh and enveloped her grandchildren in hugs. She smelled like *Cashmere Bouquet* powder. I remember my granddad, Francis (Frank) Clement Humphrey, as a quiet man. Since I am the oldest grandchild, I shortened Granddad to Dad when I started talking.

My parents: Margaret Lucy Montella, Dec 17, 1912 – April 24, 1987 and
John Kenneth Humphrey, May 6, 1915 – August 30, 1990

Inset: Dad as a young man.

My paternal grandparents:
Francis Clement Humphrey, August 18, 1890 – March 17, 1965
and Kathryn Agnes Dunn, December 8, 1891 – March 2, 1981

At least once a month, our family made the drive from Bristol to New Britain to have Sunday dinner with my grandparents. I'd sit on Dad's lap and he'd read the funnies to me. We laughed a lot. He was thin and boney, while Grammy was soft and squishy.

Dad always washed the dinner dishes, and I dried them. I asked him once why he always washed the dishes and he said, "It's quieter when I do them." I remember one of the jokes he told me. "I worked with a man by the name of John Schitz. He didn't like his name, so he changed it to Paul."

I kept a few cards that my grandparents sent me after I was married and moved away. They were all signed "Love, Grammy and Dad."

4.

Mommy, Mom, Mother, Ma

Our relationship was defined by how I addressed her. At first, I called her Mommy. I was a precocious child. I walked home from kindergarten one day when I was four because my aunt was late picking me up. Halfway home, I introduced myself to the policeman at a major street crossing. He said he was Officer Bill and he'd watch out for me. When I arrived home, Mommy and Zizi were canning tomatoes. Bursting with pride, I blurted, "I walked home all by myself." I did not expect the scolding that followed.

Any remaining self-confidence was squashed a few months later. My uncle sat me on top of the refrigerator with a bar of soap in my mouth for sassing him. "Mommy save me," I cried. She left the kitchen.

Me on a pony. Popular in the 1940s.

In grade school, she was Mom. My younger sister, Sue, always got in trouble. I'd get punished along with her because I was older and "should have known better." Mom thought that to treat us fairly, she had to treat us equally. I asked for a three-wheel chain-drive bicycle for Christmas but was told I had to be eight years old. When it arrived the following Christmas, there were two bikes – one for my sister, who was only six.

From 12 years on, I was the responsible one. Mom went to work as a nurse on the night shift and I had to take care of my one-year-old brother Jack, do the laundry and ironing, and have dinner ready by the time Daddy got home from work.

As a teenager, I spoke up for myself, but only when I knew I couldn't be heard.

"Judy, on your way to the library, drop this dish off at your aunt's house." My aunt lived on the other side of town from the library.

"Mo–ther!" I'd respond sotto voce.

"What?"

"Nothing."

In my 20s, Mother sounded too formal and I began calling her Ma.

For as long as I remember, Ma was a two-pack-a-day smoker. Many years later, when I visited Ma with my children. they were learning in grade school that smoking was bad for your health. They stole her cigarettes, broke them in half and put them back in the pack. She was so angry. I held my breath as I knew her anger could turn into screaming and yelling.

My mother and father on their wedding day, June 11, 1941

Inset: Margaret Montella, nurse at Bristol Hospital

Instead, she went outside to cool down. Ma's grandkids had a safe place in her heart not afforded to her kids.

Ma died at the age of 75 from cancer. She didn't get to meet her great-grandchildren.

She looked at me from her deathbed and said, "Promise me you'll take your name back."

"I promise, Ma." While I couldn't forgive her for what she'd done, a part of me still loved her.

Then she asked, "Was I a good mother?"

"Ma, you were the best mother that you could be." That was the only answer I could give her.

5.

First and Only

I met Edmund O'Reilly in 1957, my freshman year of high school. He was a sophomore in my music class. I didn't get to know him until my junior year, when we both joined the glee club. He began walking with me to rehearsals.

We had a Christmas concert coming up and rehearsals were held evenings at the theater where the performance would take place. I had my driver's license and could use my mother's car on rehearsal nights. My sister and her friends would pile into the car for a ride home. One of them was Ed's brother, Dennis. Dennis brought Ed with him.

During the holiday break, I had to write a paper on Robert Frost. Ed and I talked about our mutual appreciation of Frost. Ed owned books of his poetry which I asked to borrow.

When I called to get the poetry books, Ed asked me what I was doing New Year's Eve. I said, "My usual – babysitting. Why?" My sister, who was eavesdropping, made gestures at me, letting me know that she would cover my job.

Ed asked me out on a double date with his sister and her boyfriend. I said yes. It was my first date and I was so excited. It was a very cold evening and we got food at a drive-in and drove around town looking at Christmas decorations.

Just before midnight, his sister's boyfriend parked the car and started making out with her in the front seat. Ed and I were listening to the radio. At midnight he leaned over and kissed me. I was bundled up and my coat collar got in the way. He moved my collar and tried again. My girlfriends had told me that a kiss didn't count unless it lasted for at least 30 seconds. I was so nervous that I forgot to count.

Ed and I dated for the remainder of his senior year and he took me to his prom. After he graduated, he enlisted in the Army National Guard and left for basic training in New Jersey for six months. He completed training and came home for Christmas. I was halfway through my senior year.

We dated whenever we could. Ed had a full-time job at a factory and took college courses at night, and every other weekend he attended National Guard meetings and training. He escorted me to my senior prom.

After graduating from high school, I attended the College of Saint Rose in Albany, New York, to study music. Ed transferred to the Air Force and was stationed in Biloxi, Mississippi. We had a long-distance relationship, developed through letters and occasional phone calls. Midway through my sophomore year, Ed proposed.

The night we got engaged, I rushed home to show my mother my ring. "Huh," she said. "You could have received a bigger diamond from your grandmother." On the morning of the wedding, I had a moment alone with my mother. I asked her if she had any words of wisdom. She said, "It's not too late."

Over the years, Ed and I spent much time apart because of his military assignments which lasted from two weeks to a year. It's probably what kept us married for 14 years. I oversaw paying the bills, raising the kids, and managing the house, while Ed lived a bachelor life when he was away; and sometimes continued that lifestyle at home. Years later, when asked what went wrong with our marriage, I told people we grew up and grew apart.

Younger than Springtime,
Prom, April 1961

6.

Vase of Innocence

It was delivered
on my seventeenth birthday
Someone banged on the front door
No one ever came to the front door
Access was around the back
Even the mail was delivered around the back
I peeked through the curtains and saw a man
holding something small
It looked like flowers
"Delivery for Judy Humphrey," he said
"That's me," I said
He handed me a vase and left
The vase was formed into two hands
Six tiny pink rosebuds peeked out
The card read:
Happy Birthday with love
Simple and beautiful
Such naive times
Before all the drama and the tears of a lifetime
I have kept the vase for sixty years
To remind me of innocence and lost love

7.

The Piano – 1947 to the Present

I grew up with a piano. Daddy taught me to read music before I could read words. At four years old, I started formal lessons. I was so little that my feet didn't reach the pedals and my fingers could not reach an octave. My daily practice included finger exercises and eventually I could span ten keys. I studied piano through two years of college. In my sixties I had surgery to remove a cyst from my left hand and the surgeon asked if I had any pain in my hands because both my thumbs were dislocated!

My first piano was a seven-foot studio grand Steinway. Only the nine-foot concert grand is larger. When I married Ed, he got me a new Steinway studio upright. We made monthly payments on it for five years.

Oh, how I love that piano. But it didn't have an easy life. Shortly after we got it in Biloxi, Mississippi, the Air Force transferred Ed to Wheelus Air Base in Tripoli, Libya. The only other furniture we owned was a mattress and box spring.

The piano arrived before I did. It travelled by ship from Norfolk. It must have had a rough journey because one leg was broken, and we weren't able to get it repaired in Libya. Most of the population had never seen a piano. Ed propped it up with a piece of 4x4 he found on the base. We spent months writing letters to the Air Force, the shipping company and claims adjusters, trying to get reimbursed for the damage, to no avail.

My piano suffered other indignities. Sandstorms were frequent. Libyan sand was like fine sugar – it infiltrated everything. Black flies left specks all over it. Screens helped a little, but the flies came in through the door every time it opened. I tried to protect my piano with two layers, cloth and plastic. Whenever I removed the covers to play, I dusted off a layer of sand and dead flies.

The first villa we rented in Tripoli belonged to an Arab farmer with five children. Only the oldest boy spoke English and his job was to collect the rent. The first day our rent was due, I was playing the piano when Hamdi appeared at my door. He wanted to know where the sound was coming from and I showed him. There was sheet music open on the stand and he pointed to it and asked, "You speak this?" When I nodded, he said, "Speak now." I don't remember what I played but he stood beside me mesmerized.

The following month, he brought his siblings with him. They were fascinated. I guess their father told them not to bother the American because they never came back inside. But when they heard the piano speaking, they gathered under my window to listen.

A week before my son was born, we moved to a much smaller apartment closer to Wheelus. The piano made the trip in the back of a pick-up truck and survived with no further damage.

When we entertained friends, I played piano, but only after a couple of beers for courage. Although I had lessons for 16 years, I was always nervous performing. My piano teacher never held recitals. As a music major in college, I had to perform twice a year for my grade. I got so upset that for a week before a concert, I was unable to eat or sleep. The hall would be empty except for the music faculty who sat in the back row with their red pens, jotting down comments and grading my performance. I lived in fear of sneezing in the middle of a concert, or worse, forgetting the piece.

My piano underwent one final trauma in Libya. Moving day for our trip home was during Ramadan, a month-long time of fasting, prayer and reflection. From sunrise to sunset, Muslims do not eat or drink, use tobacco or have sexual relations. Consequently, our movers stayed up half the night to compensate. It was difficult for them to work in the hot sun without anything to sustain their energy. Seven men hoisted the piano, wobbling toward the moving van. Just as they got there, they dropped it, shattering its remaining leg. While the men yelled and cursed at each other in Arabic, Ed gathered wood and constructed a crate into which he had the men haul the piano. He then bolted the piano to the crate, bolstered the keyboard, protected it with padding, and nailed the whole thing shut.

Five months later, we received our furniture in our new home in Klamath Falls, Oregon. When the movers brought the crate in, one asked, "What the hell you got in there, Buddy – a friggin' motorcycle?" Nope, just a piano. From then on, every time we moved, my piano travelled in style in its own crate.

It took two years and three more moves before we were reimbursed for the legs. We ordered two replacement legs from Steinway. I stained them to match the piano and Ed installed them. We moved 17 times in 14 years and the piano survived.

Each time we settled in a new place, I taught piano lessons in my home. When Mike and Maureen started school, I tried to teach them to play the piano. They learned how to read music but would not accept me as their teacher. Nothing I did worked. I even tried going outside and knocking on the door.

"Your teacher is here. It's time for your lesson," I said.

"You're not our teacher, you're our mom."

Mike fell in love with the violin in 3rd grade. Maureen took up flute and piccolo in 6th grade. I still play my piano.

8.

Hands

Part I

Hands are very telling of bodily age
A newborn's hands are closed into tiny fists
They say "I'm not ready to let you in yet"
What a thrill to nudge that little fist
Only to have him grab onto your finger
And hold tight
A baby's hands are chubby
With dimples on the knuckles
He opens them readily to feel things
And pick them up
When the dimples disappear, he's no longer a baby
But a trusting toddler learning to walk
He squeezes your hand
Knowing you will keep him safe
When he starts school, you hold his hand
While crossing streets or
In a crowd so he does not get lost
Almost overnight he doesn't need to hold your hand anymore
But wistfully, perhaps you still need to hold his
Then one day, he is holding another's hand
So much in love.
Soon there is another baby's fist to coax open
To grab your finger
And so it goes

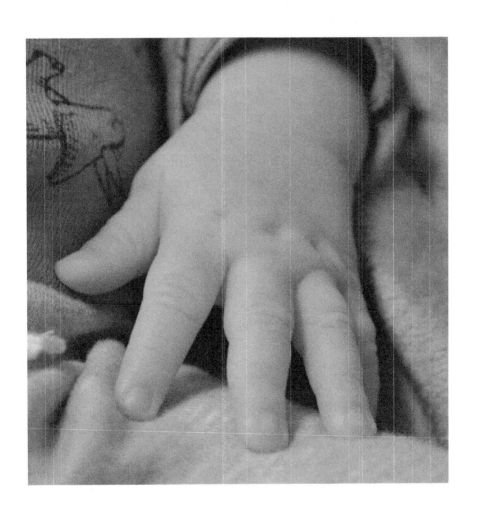

Part II

My hands are small with short fingers
Not the hands of a pianist
Still, I began lessons at four years old
Stretching my fingers daily to reach an octave
Over time, my fingers and hands grew stronger
Years later I found excessive stretching
Had dislocated both my thumbs
But I could reach an octave plus two
My hands went from pretty and smooth
To calloused with bleeding knuckles
From washing diapers by hand in my 20s
When income permitted modern conveniences
My hands regained their previous appearance
With the help of hand cream used regularly
Much later, in my 50s, or was it my 60s
My hands looked wrinkled
Nails broke occasionally
And hangnails sprouted overnight
No longer could I wear my rings
My fingers swelled with heat or altitude
Arthritis attacked some knuckles and
My hands were no longer pretty
In my 70s now I still use hand cream daily
And play the piano and knit and write
"I love holding your hands" Granddaughter said
"They're so soft and warm"
And so they are

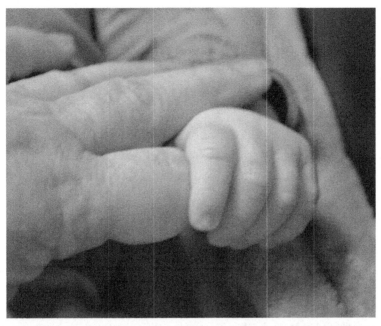

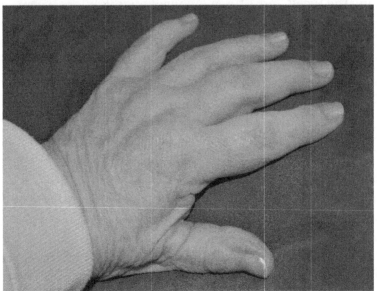

9.

Albany, New York – St. Rose 1961

During my first two years of college, I was a rosebud – the name given to undergraduates at the College of St. Rose. It was an all-girls Catholic college run by the Sisters of Saint Joseph. It was my first time away from my family. I was accepted into the music program after passing an audition on the piano.

The rules were strict. Ladies always wore nylon hose. Socks were permitted but only over the nylons. Pants were not allowed. Skirt and dress hems ended below the knee. We wore knee length uniforms for gym classes. Lights out was 10 p.m. during the week and 11 p.m. on weekends. Seniors were allowed a midnight curfew on Friday and Saturday. The only men allowed in the dorm rooms were fathers and brothers, and only on moving days. Dates were permitted with prior parental approval. The meeting area for a date was the common room in the dorm. It was aptly called the goldfish bowl because it had windows on three sides. A nun monitored the sign-out desk.

Any infraction of the rules resulted in being restricted to the campus for a week. My friends and I obeyed the rules without question. We didn't want to risk losing the freedom to go to a movie or to an afternoon dance at nearby Rensselaer Polytechnic Institute. Even then we had to travel in groups of three or more.

In high school, I was a National Honor Society member. Every morning when my dad dropped me off at school he would say, "Don't work too hard, but get all A's." I felt I was a failure if I got a B.

Unlike high school, some of my college classes were a struggle. Most of my classmates were from New York and had studied history for four years. Connecticut required only one year. I barely passed my history class. I did well in my music classes, including piano lessons. However, having no experience playing in piano recitals, I suffered from performance anxiety.

During my second year at St. Rose, I volunteered to teach music at the orphanage near the college. I had taught piano to younger children while living at home. Teaching music in a classroom was more difficult. I did not enjoy the experience and began to question my career path. From a young age, every time someone had asked me what I wanted to be when I grew up, I had answered a music teacher. My mother taught me that response. It was years before I realized that was her dream, not mine.

At the end of my sophomore year, I quit to marry Ed, my high school sweetheart and the only boy I'd ever dated. He was in the Air Force and we moved around a lot, so I lost track of my college friends.

Though I didn't graduate with my class, I was invited to attend its 50th reunion in 2012. A former roommate had tracked me down. The women I knew as teenagers had formed strong bonds and were still close friends. After graduation, they worked as teachers, married other Catholics for life, bought homes, had children, became active in their church parishes and volunteered.

In the reunion booklet, classmates included photos of their weddings, family, or their yearbook image. I sent a picture of myself standing near a helicopter in Hawaii, hair blowing, camera in hand. To my classmates I was a curiosity. The life I lived was foreign to them. Though parts of my life were difficult, I wouldn't trade it for anything.

Part 2

Tripoli

10.

Designation: Dep-w

When I married Ed, I didn't know that there would be three entities in the union: Ed, me, and the United States Air Force. The pecking order was Ed, Ed's career, Ed's car, Ed's tools, Ed's hobbies, Ed's friends, his children, and oh, his wife. He always introduced me as "my wife." I had no name. The Air Force did not acknowledge my name either. I had a designation: dep-w, dependent wife. I was listed under Ed's name and service number. The prevalent military thought was that if the Army/Navy/Air Force wanted you to have a wife, they would have issued you one.

Military wives were not allowed to work outside of the home except with permission from the base commander and only in certain jobs such as secretary or nurse. Everything a wife did was put on her husband's record. If a wife got a speeding ticket, it was placed on the husband's record and counted against his promotion. Military men were encouraged to keep their wives under control. It was not unusual to see a woman sporting a black eye or two.

Another tenet of military life was R.H.I.P. Rank has its privileges. Medical care was doled out to wives based on the rank of their husbands. If ten women had a nine o'clock appointment, the one with the highest-ranking husband would be seen first regardless of the seriousness of the illness or what time she arrived.

20-year-old bride, July 1, 1963

We were married on July 1. Ed was stationed in Biloxi, Mississippi. I was a 20-year-old bride living in my own home in what seemed like a foreign country. It was 1963 and John F. Kennedy was the president.

We lived in a three-room house off the base; bedroom, bathroom, and everything-else room. The house was already inhabited – by cockroaches, mosquitoes and lizards. I managed to vanquish the mosquitoes and lizards, but the cockroaches were there to stay. My mother had told me that only lousy housekeepers would get cockroaches. That wasn't true in the south. Everyone had roaches. I think they were the first inhabitants of Mississippi. They were immune to bug spray.

Segregation abounded in Mississippi, as did confederate flags and weekly revivals. Because of my Yankee upbringing, I was confused by local practices. I thought the Civil War ended and Lincoln freed the slaves. I didn't understand the difference between "colored trash" and "white trash." To me garbage was garbage no matter what color it was. I don't recall seeing any United States flags displayed, only Confederate flags. I wondered if the people pledged allegiance to the Confederacy instead of to the United States of America. I never found out what was being revived under the revival tents each weekend.

Our street had an elementary school at one end and a high school at the other. No regular classes were held on Fridays because children were taught to worship football every Friday. Participation was mandatory as a member of the team, the cheerleading squad, the pep club, or the band.

Our neighborhood housed a few other young military couples. The wives banded together to share trips to buy groceries at the base commissary. No one had extra money.

Most of the wives were pregnant. When I got pregnant, I felt like I belonged.

Ed received orders for a transfer to Tripoli, Libya. We didn't know if I would be allowed to go with him. I started getting all the vaccinations I would need for the trip: typhoid, typhus, yellow fever, diphtheria, tetanus, polio, smallpox, measles, and a test for tuberculosis. One of the vaccines contributed to the miscarriage I had at three and a half months. That was to be my first experience with military healthcare.

I started passing blood clots. The doctor ordered bed rest for two weeks. When the bleeding worsened, Ed took me to the hospital. The reason for my admission was "incomplete abortion." I was Catholic; I couldn't have an abortion. I was terrified. I had never been in a hospital. They put me in a ward with 11 other patients, separated only by curtains. It was past midnight, and all the other patients were asleep. Nurses told me not to wake anyone up. I had an IV in my arm. It hurt. So did my belly. Silent tears ran down my face soaking my pillow. No one checked on me all night.

At dawn, a nurse came to see me. My arm was swollen and discolored. The nurse said the IV had infiltrated; the fluid missed my vein and went under my skin.

I had to use the bedpan. I refused the soiled one the nurse brought, and when I finally sat on one, I passed what I thought was a large blood clot. It was my baby. It had been dead for three weeks. Then I started crying out loud.

The nurse brought me to a treatment room where the doctor performed a Dilation and Curettage. With no anesthesia. Ed heard me screaming on his way in to visit me. When the doctor finished the procedure, he told me to walk back to my room. I could barely sit up. Ed helped me get back into bed.

The next day I was home recuperating. After an afternoon nap, I turned the radio on to listen to music. Every station was playing soft soothing music, no talking, no commercials. A voice came on and announced, "The President is dead. President John Fitzgerald Kennedy is dead."

11.

Arrival and Birth

Luke, Chapter 2, Verse 7: And she brought forth her firstborn son, and wrapped him in swaddling clothes, and laid him in a manger, because there was no room for them in the inn.

I was three months pregnant when I got off the plane in Libya on April 8, 1964. The first thing I noticed was the heat. I travelled from snow in Connecticut to an oven in Libya. The heat was oppressive and I couldn't catch my breath.

Ed was not in the group of people waiting on the tarmac. Passengers were ushered into a small building which wasn't much cooler. I had an urge to run back to the air-conditioned plane. Distracted by the heat, I didn't recognize Ed in a white linen suit, showing off his tan.

Ed drove me home – a villa complex 17 miles inland from Wheelus Air Force Base. Our car had no air-conditioning.

The second thing I noticed was the smell. It was nauseating – a mixture of rotting tomatoes, rotting dates, animal and human excrement, and the dusty scent of fine sand. The heat seemed to enhance the odors.

The countryside reminded me of bible stories. Date palm trees grew along the Mediterranean coast. Camels and donkeys were used for transportation.

I hadn't believed the bible story about the crown of thorns; the only thorns I knew were on roses. The bushes in Libya produced six-inch-long thorns that looked more like spikes, and farms were ringed with thorn bushes to keep in animals.

Aerial view of East Gate Farm, Tagiura, Libya.
Our unit – our second residence – is one in from the end, marked with an 'x'

Our villa was part of a five-unit complex built around a central courtyard. We lived next door to the Arab landlord, who spoke no English, and his family. The other three units were occupied by families from the southern US. At night, bats flew through clotheslines in the courtyard as if testing their sonar.

The building was made of sandstone blocks. The ceilings were ten feet high and the heat hid near the ceiling during the day only to descend upon us at night. The windows had shutters that we kept closed against the heat. The coolest place was on the cement-tile floor and I laid on the floor until my body heated the spot under me. Then I'd roll over to another spot.

When Ed first arrived at the base, he shared a room in the barracks. After I arrived, we invited his roommate and his wife over for dinner. We became good friends and often visited in each other's homes.

One day, the neighborhood women – other air force wives – were talking in the courtyard when I went out to hang my laundry. When they saw me, they left without talking to me. Later, I caught one of them alone in the courtyard and asked why none of them spoke to me.

"You had some of those people in your house," she said.

I said, "Oh, you mean our friends Bob and Shirley? Yes, they came over for dinner."

"What? You let them eat off your dishes?" She slammed her door. Bob and Shirley were from Jamaica. My southern white American neighbors never spoke to me again during the five months we lived there.

Later, we moved closer to the base to a complex of 17 units, owned by an Italian who spoke English, and we had a party for our friends who'd helped us move. We ate my homemade pizza and drank beer, which cost less than Coke. The next morning, I awoke with gas pains and Ed took me to the hospital. I wasn't due for three weeks.

On September 8, 1964, I brought forth my newborn son, Michael Joseph O'Reilly, and lay him in a laundry basket because there were no cribs at the base exchange.

12.

It's a Girl

Pregnant. Again. So soon. That wasn't supposed to happen. The doctor said I couldn't get pregnant while breast feeding. He lied. Mike was only three months old. I had not yet had a period.

The doctor said the baby was due in mid-October. He lied again. Maureen Ann O'Reilly was born August 15, 1965 and was full term. Our Arab landlord sent condolences. Only the birth of sons was celebrated in Libya.

Maureen had dark hair. Another condolence. You could get more money for a blonde baby on the black market.

Arab women were acknowledged only when they gave birth to a son. Otherwise, they were to remain out of sight, completely covered by clothing except for their hands and one eye. If a male family member caught them out of the house with their face uncovered, they would be punished.

Our landlord had five children – two boys and three girls. Two of the girls were teens. The youngest was five. Whenever one of the girls had her period, the other two were locked in a room with her for the duration. They were considered unclean.

The girls had nothing to do in confinement. They sent the five-year-old through the window on the courtyard to beg for things from the Americans – needles and thread, buttons, paper and pencils, chocolate.

Shortly after Maureen was born, Ed was sent on a mission for two months. In fact, he spent most of her first year away – in Nigeria, Mauritius, Ascension Island. He was part of an Air Rescue Squadron which was deployed around the world whenever NASA launched a space shuttle. In the early days of the space program, the capsules did not land but splashed down in the ocean. If all went well, the capsule would be retrieved off the coast of Florida. If not, there were squadrons standing by to retrieve it wherever it landed.

Maureen didn't get to know her dad until she was over a year old. During his short visits between assignments, she shied away from him. It wasn't until her doll's head fell off that she approached Ed on her own. "Daddy, fix Dolly, pweeze," she said. He got his tools and reattached the doll's head. He gave the doll back to her and she hugged his knees. It's the only time I ever saw tears in his eyes.

Near the end of our stay in Libya, the base commander presented me and the other squadron wives with plaques commemorating our service. I still have mine. I think it belongs to my daughter now.

13.

Living in Libya – 1966

Temperatures rarely dipped below 80 degrees, even at night, and I slept on a bath towel to absorb my perspiration and keep the sheets dry.

There were a few variations in temperature – hot (80 degrees and up), extremely hot (120 to 130 degrees) and hot with wind. Ghibli winds carried sand from the Sahara Desert and the sand was exceptionally fine, like gritty powder that you could grind between your teeth. Occasionally, the Ghibli collided with wind carrying moisture from the Mediterranean Sea, causing mud to fall from the sky.

Every December it rained non-stop for three weeks, the only rain the country would get in a year. Our first December, the roof leaked around the edges of each room. We told the landlord.

"I can't fix the roof; it's raining," he said.

When the rain stopped, he said, "I can't fix the roof; I can't see any leaks." That was the Libyan way.

We were given salt tablets to make us drink more so we wouldn't dehydrate. However, the water tasted like chemical-laden sea water. Milk was available. It was reconstituted – powdered milk mixed with water and added vitamins. It was called *Sterovita*. It tasted awful. I drank lots of *Coca-Cola*. It was bottled in the States.

Potable water for drinking, cooking, and bathing the kids, was available on the base. Every few days I filled our seven-gallon jug.

The water that was piped into the house came from a well that served 17 American families and the landlord. It was wet, warm, salty, and full of bugs and sand. It was pumped into an open holding tank for distribution. I kept a sock on the spigot to strain the sand and bugs out. I added bleach to the water before using it to wash dishes and diapers. My hands were raw from the bleach.

We lost electricity when it rained or the wind blew, and on Fridays. When we had electricity, the current constantly fluctuated. Light bulbs would dim and brighten, and occasionally a bulb broke from too much current.

Some people had television sets which they plugged into a regulator so the current wouldn't blow out the tubes. Ed made extra money repairing TVs. I'd watch a TV set for an hour after he repaired it to make sure it worked. We didn't own one.

Since the electricity was so unstable, I kept our food cold in an ice box. I bought blocks of ice from the base.

All our food was shipped from the States and was old when we got it. Meat was frozen for so long that sometimes the edges of a steak would be tinged in green. Eggs were kept in cold storage. Once, Ed had inventory duty at the commissary and he found cartons of eggs stamped 1943, from WW II. Only seven out of a dozen eggs were usable. I had to crack an egg into a separate bowl first to make sure it wasn't black or hairy. If I fried an egg in butter, it would just lay in the pan – no crackling.

All the dry goods – cereal, flour, bread and pasta – were full of bugs. When I poured pasta into boiling water, I had to skim the bugs that floated to the top. Fresh bread was available but was made with the buggy flour. I picked the large bug bodies out of the bread then toasted it before eating so I couldn't see the small bugs I missed. I suppose they added protein to our diet.

Fresh produce was not so fresh by the time we got it. I recall people fighting over heads of lettuce, which were mostly brown. Once during our three years there, each family was given one full grocery bag of fresh oranges. What a treat! I ended up with sores around my mouth from eating so many before they rotted.

During my two pregnancies spent in Tripoli, I dreamed of eating fresh crisp lettuce, of biting into a juicy ripe tomato or a sweet fresh apple. Because of the lack of palatable food, I gained only 12 pounds with my son, and 10 pounds with my daughter who weighed seven pounds at birth.

Occasionally, the landlord would sell us fresh eggs from his chickens. The eggs had bright orange yolks because the hens were fed table scraps, but they tasted better than the cold storage eggs.

One of the smells that upset my stomach, especially during pregnancy, was rotting tomatoes. Tomatoes were smashed and spread on a plank to dry in the sun. To this day, I cannot tolerate sun-dried tomatoes, even though they are not covered in flies like they were in Libya.

Fortunately, I was able to breastfeed my babies until they were four months old, before they had to drink *Sterovita*. *Gerber* baby food was available in the commissary.

I cooked on a propane stove in the kitchen. When the heat was unbearable, I used a charcoal grill outside, which presented the added challenge of keeping flies off the food.

Pesky black flies were everywhere. I once hung a sticky fly strip inside the porch near the door, hoping to capture them before they got into the house. Two hours later it was coated. So many flies trying to escape the strip made it sway and hum.

Libyan flies were slow though – must have been the heat. If you brushed a fly off your hand, it would make a slow circle and land back in the same spot. We never bought food at the nearby open-air market – it came with a side of flies.

Libyans were plagued with eye diseases. Flies lived in the corners of children's eyes and under their noses. It was unusual to see a flyless child.

I washed diapers in a wringer washer at 4 a.m. when no one else was using the electricity, and hung them outdoors on a long clothesline. By the time I got them all hung, I could begin to take them down because they'd be dry. If I didn't take the diapers in before the sun rose, the flies would cover them with specks.

Before going to bed each night, I had fly patrol. When the sun set, the flies settled down for the night. I stalked them with my trusty flyswatter, usually killing seven or more. I hated being awakened by flies crawling over my face.

Flies left evidence everywhere they landed, in the form of little black specks. When we returned to the States, antiqued furniture was the rage. New furniture was painted with little black dots to make it look old. The few pieces of furniture we owned accumulated the specks naturally. I spent hours cleaning them off. I never bought a piece of antiqued furniture.

Dinner at the NCO Club, 1966

14.

House Guests

Besides flies, which were annoying, other bugs in Libya were scary. I thought the cockroaches in Mississippi were bad. Libyan roaches were four times bigger.

One afternoon I found Maureen sitting on the bathroom floor calling, "Mommy, buggy, buggy." Roaches poured out of the floor drain. Ed in his combat boots stomped on the bugs till they were all dead. What a mess! My job was to clean up after the bug slayer. We poured a can of bug killer down the drain and covered the opening with a metal cap.

Occasional visitors included spiders so large they hopped instead of crawled, hissing lizards that looked like miniature dinosaurs, and scorpions. The deadliest were the black scorpions. If they bit a child, the child would die.

I used floor wax that contained a bug killer. I didn't want the kids crawling on the poisoned floor, so I confined them to a playpen.

The floor wax was effective. I found a dead scorpion under the couch. The poison must have taken some time to work because one night I found a live scorpion under my bed. I had a bedside lamp on the floor next to the bed so I could see my way back after a 2 a.m. feeding. I heard scratching and found a six-inch long scorpion stuck between the lamp and the bed. I woke Ed who grabbed a kitchen knife and chopped the scorpion into five pieces. It was my job to clean up after the bug slayer.

Libya was also home to a deadly snake that we called the "bet-you-can't-count-to ten" snake because, if bitten, you would be dead before you could count to ten. I think it was a black mamba. I never saw one, which made me feel both safe and uneasy.

Besides flies, and us, ants populated the house. I think they lived in the walls which were made of limestone blocks. They mysteriously appeared under the tapestries we hung on the 12-foot-high walls, and to get rid of them, I vacuumed them live off the wall. When I emptied the vacuum bag, it practically walked itself to the trash.

One day, two hours after I'd used the bathroom, I went back in and the walls and ceiling were crawling with ants. It was a full-scale invasion. Ed set a can of *Raid* on the floor, taped it to the *ON* position and shut the door. An hour later, we opened the door, and the room was dripping with *Raid* and dead ants. This was a worse mess than the roaches. I of course had to clean up after the bug slayer.

Another creature made a single appearance – a tiny mouse. There was only one electric outlet in the bedroom which we used for the bedside lamp. When we got a fan, Ed punched a small hole in the wall above our bed to run a wire through to the outlet on the porch. In the middle of the night, he woke me yelling, "Cut it out!" I thought he was dreaming. "Stop it!" he said.

"Stop what?"

"Stop throwing sand in my face!" I turned the light on. There was a mouse perched at the edge of the hole in the wall, digging his way through. Too tired to get up, Ed stabbed the mouse with a pencil. My job, in the morning – dispose of the shish-ka-mouse.

15.

Rattus

I killed a rat once.

I became a daily killer in Tripoli – ants, flies, mice, cockroaches, but a rat? It was huge; over a foot long minus the tail. It had beady black, dead eyes, even before it was dead. It crawled onto my porch under the door.

A few days before the sighting, I found mouse droppings on the porch. Because they were slightly larger than usual, I baited two mouse traps from my supply. I would do anything to protect my children.

Late one afternoon I heard a sharp crack, followed by a flap-scrape, flap-scrape sound. I eased the front door open and saw a rat heading for the porch door. It was dragging a trap clamped to one foot. It turned its black eyes toward me. I panicked and grabbed the first thing I saw – a hammer on Ed's work bench. I swung it and hit the rat on the head. It stopped. Fearing I'd only knocked it out, I hit it a couple more times. No movement, no twitching. Then my knees turned to jelly.

I would do anything to protect my children.

16.

A Different Kind of Life

Besides bugs and small critters, some human behaviors were difficult to deal with.

It was so hot that the entire country shut down between noon and 3 p.m. During this time, groups of men sat in the shade of palm trees, around a small fire, cooking tea – shaei in Arabic. Tea leaves were boiled in a small amount of water for 20 minutes. A generous amount of sugar was added until the tea resembled a thick syrup. Women were not allowed to participate.

1965
BLESSINGS
at Christmas

Tripoli, Libya

Men relieved themselves in public whenever they felt the need. They considered the entire outdoors as their bathroom. Their houses had no bathing facilities. Little children ran around naked while women had to cover their entire bodies.

Ed and I had to take a driving course to get our Libyan driver's licenses. What we really learned was how to navigate obstacles. The obstacles were pedestrians, animals, bicycles, carts, wheelbarrows. All had the right of way. At an intersection, the one who took up the most room – a camel for instance – would have the right of way. Next in order was a truck, followed by a car with the loudest horn, other wheeled vehicles, and two or four legged creatures. Stop signs were interpreted to mean step on the gas, lean on your horn, and plow through.

At times, stopping was dangerous. Once, a cyclist rode so close to our Volkswagen bus that when we stopped, he ran into our side mirror and knocked it off with his head.

The Air Force held meetings every three months to remind us that we were guests in Libya. Families were instructed on preparedness. In case we had to be evacuated, we were supposed to have a suitcase packed for each member of the family with clothes and food for a week. I had two kids in diapers which I had to wash every two days. There were no *Pampers* in the 60s. None of the families we knew could afford the extra clothing it would take to be prepared.

Fortunately, we didn't have to deal with an evacuation, but our friends did. We left Libya in January 1967. In June, the Arab-Israeli Six Day War took place between Israel, Jordan, Syria and Egypt. Though Libya was not directly involved, Libyans stormed the base in protest.

The children attending the base school at the time were put on a plane to Germany. Most of the enlisted men and their families lived off the base though. The families were picked up by the police with nothing but the clothes on their backs. Belongings and even pets were left behind. Some people had to be evacuated from the beach by helicopter. Families were reunited in Germany then sent back to the States. Our friends still living in Libya lost everything they owned.

17.

The Cement Mixer

His name was Masood. He was six feet tall and black as coal. He didn't know much English, but he always had a smile and he was friendly with the kids who lived in the complex. He always made them laugh and they followed him around the farm as he did his work. He had a wife and five children of his own.

Ed wanted to put a cement patio in front of our house to keep out the sand and provide solid ground for our barbeque and picnic table. He asked the landlord if he could borrow his cement mixer. The landlord sent Masood with a shovel.

Ed leveled the ground and laid out string where he wanted the patio poured. Masood dug a hole in the middle of the area, emptied a bag of cement, added water and sand and mixed it with the shovel. He worked for hours in the sun mixing and spreading without even a water break.

When he was finished, Ed was going to give him a carton of cigarettes as payment. Libyans could trade American cigarettes on the black market for anything – it was better than cash. The landlord said to give Masood only one pack of cigarettes because a carton would spoil him. Ed slipped him two packs, and I wrapped some food for him to take because I'd seen him searching through the garbage cans for scraps.

18.

Road Trips in Libya

A paved road stretched ten kilometers along the Mediterranean Sea between Wheelus Air Force Base and Tripoli. The Arabs call Wheelus 'Malaha' which means salt flats. The base was built around an abandoned area where the sea was channeled inland to evaporate so that salt could be collected, a practice dating to Roman times when salt was currency.

One day, Ed and I were going to explore the old quarter of Tripoli. Few vehicles were on the road, but traffic picked up as we neared the downtown area, and motor bikes and bicyclists competed for limited space, making our trip hazardous. I was happy Ed was driving.

As we worked our way through the open market – the Sukh ('sook') – the cobblestone roads got narrower. The old quarter was surrounded by a high stone wall built in the second century by the Romans; we drove through the gate surrounded by pedestrians and vehicles. We should have begun our trip at noon when the country shut down for three hours during the hottest part of the day.

On the road's wide shoulder, two men created rugs from animal skins. I had seen sheepskin rugs for sale but had no idea how they were made. The men nailed the skin to a board, fur side down. They then wet the back and spread a mixture of white powder and water evenly over it. They propped the board with skin attached against a wall to dry in the sun.

Normally we could not take pictures of people because the Arabs believed that the camera would steal their soul, but the two craftsmen cheerfully posed for us with the finished rugs.

We followed the perimeter wall of the old city which eventually turned inland. While heading toward the exit, we ended in an alley so narrow that the side mirror of the car scraped the building and we had to back up. A group of children playing nearby started taunting us. They picked up rocks and threw them at the car and spat at us. Ed drove as quickly as he could without hitting anyone while I cowered in the passenger seat. We made it through the gate, at which point the children broke off their pursuit. In our three years in Libya, we never went back to the old quarter.

However, we did explore the Roman ruins of Sabratha, 43 miles west of Tripoli; and Leptis Magna, 81 miles east. Sabratha was in better shape and its open-air theater was used for plays and other entertainment.

On the trip to Leptis Magna, we had to carry a can of gas. There was nothing but sand between Tripoli and Leptis. About halfway, we came over a rise and saw a large encampment of Bedouins. Camels, goats, and children roamed freely, ignoring our passage.

Leptis was not as well excavated or preserved as Sabratha. It was a larger site and it also included a theater, half buried in sand. The racetrack in the amphitheater was not fully excavated and archways were haphazardly put together, rendering their Latin inscriptions unreadable. One structure was recognizable – a communal toilet. Two rows of stone holes faced each other. Troughs ran beneath and exited out of the building. There were no roofs or doors.

The Libyan ruins were not tourist attractions like the Colosseum and Forum in Rome. We saw a few visitors in Sabratha but none in Leptis Magna.

On our trip back along the coast road, we saw nothing but sand. The large encampment had disappeared, leaving no trace, not even hoof or footprints. Maybe it was a mirage.

Ruins of Roman amphitheater at Leptis Magna, Libya, July 1964

19.

I Hope I Get Out of Here Alive

Ed's tour of duty ended in January 1967. Leaving Tripoli was more complicated than arriving. The two of us began our life in Libya with a bed, a piano, and kitchen items. Three years later, there were four of us and a houseful of furniture.

The military began processing paperwork in November for the January move. We were moving from a desert climate at sea level to Klamath Falls, Oregon, elevation 4000 feet. Living with four distinct seasons would prove challenging.

I usually dressed Mike and Maureen in diapers, shirts and shoes. It was too hot for any more clothing. Trying one-piece snow suits on them was difficult. The kids cried the whole time, standing with their arms stuck out at their sides, sweating and afraid to move. Mike at two years old and Maureen at one had never experienced a temperature below 80 degrees. We were flying to New York in the middle of winter. There would be a lot more crying.

The kids and I spent our last two weeks in Libya on the base in transitional housing – two bedrooms connected by a bathroom. There were no cooking facilities and we had to walk six blocks to the café to get food. Ed worked until the day before we left. During the second week, I got sick – fever, chills, vomiting, diarrhea – I could hardly stand up. Forget about trips to get food. Also, there were no telephones. I stayed on the bathroom floor to be close to the toilet and still watch the kids in their bedroom.

I must have dozed off at one point as I awoke to the sounds of the kids laughing and I crawled into their room to check on them. They had found the *Diaperene*, a cream I used on them to prevent diaper rash. They had emptied the tube, spreading the cream over each other, and finger painting it on the dresser and mirror. I crawled back to the bathroom floor. I felt too sick to do anything. Besides, they were having fun.

As I lay there, I prayed, "Please God, don't let me die here – on a bathroom floor – in a foreign country."

Fortunately, when Ed came in from work, he took one look at me and carried me to bed. He bathed and fed the kids and cleaned everything up. I passed out and slept until the next morning. I survived.

Part III

Marriage & Divorce

20.

Kill Her in Klamath Falls

There was a sign on Highway 140 in Oregon heading south toward Nevada: *Save money. Don't divorce your wife in Reno. Kill her in Klamath Falls.*

In 1967, Klamath Falls had a per capita murder rate that rivaled big cities. Most of the killings were of Native Americans, by Native Americans, when they came from the reservation to the town bars in the evenings.

Ed and I were safe living on the other side of town near the Air Force Base. And we never went out in the evenings.

Our time in Oregon was a blur. We lived there for a year in three different homes. The first was a furnished mobile home, because our belongings were still in transit from Libya. Next, we bought a ranch house with sweat equity for a down payment. We installed the subfloor and painted the building inside and out with a primer and two topcoats. I stained all the trim and Ed installed the lighting.

We worked on the house evenings and weekends. By the time I got to bed, I was exhausted. I dreamed of nailing and painting. My arm moved in my sleep as if I were still using a brush.

All-electric homes were in vogue then but keeping the house warm was a strain on our budget. We could afford to heat only the bathroom and the kids' bedroom. We had a circulating fireplace that kept the living room and kitchen warm, but the heat didn't reach our bedroom at the end of the hall.

Ed put up plastic storm windows. After a week, he said he needed fresh air to sleep and tore the plastic and opened the window in our bedroom two inches. I was freezing. I wore mittens and a ski hat to bed.

The next morning, snow was piled in the corner of the bedroom. I had to shovel it out before doing my next chore – relighting the fire and piling on more logs so the house would be warm enough for Ed to get up for work.

In the spring, Ed was accepted into the Air Force program that would lead to a college degree and officer rank. We put the house on the market and it sold quickly. We rented another house for two months until we were again relocated, this time to California.

I didn't completely unpack our belongings from Tripoli until we rented a house in Sacramento.

21.

Sacramento Blues – 1968

After relocating three times in Klamath Falls, it was nice to settle in Sacramento where Ed would be stationed for the next three years.

The Air Force enrolled him at Sacramento State University to study civil engineering. Ed got a good deal. He would get his degree and a promotion to officer rank in return for two years of service for each year of school.

Sacramento was paradise compared to the other places we'd lived. The temperature was moderate year-round. There were three growing seasons. We had a large vegetable garden and several fruit trees in our yard. Roses bloomed in December. And there were no bugs.

We lived close to the college but had access to two Air Force bases for shopping and medical care. Many cultural venues were available in the area. We were within a two-hour drive of San Francisco.

I became super homemaker – freezing fruits and vegetables, making pies and jam, keeping the house spotless, managing the bills. However, I longed for intellectual stimulation. Ed spent his time in classes and study groups. We had only one car. I was homebound.

Mike and Maureen started school at Ethel Phillips Elementary, one of the first bilingual schools in California. Because of the influx of migrant workers from Mexico into the

Sacramento valley to harvest the crops, the school taught half a day of Spanish and half a day of English for kindergarten, first and second grades. Caucasian children were the minority. Parents were invited to take bilingual classes in the evenings.

My introduction to Mexican food came at the first Cinco de Maio celebration. It was a potluck dinner held at the school. The Mexican parents brought their specialty dishes, handed down for generations. I knew nothing about Mexican food, so I brought a green salad. The food was delicious and spicy. I have loved Mexican food ever since.

Ed's college courses were mostly in engineering and math. He had to take an English course which required several book reports. I lived vicariously by reading all the books and writing the reports for him. I enjoyed doing that and wished I could take courses too. I had quit college after two years to get married.

He also had to fulfill a physical education requirement and signed up for Tai Kwon Do, signing me up as well. At first, I was angry with him because I spent my high school years avoiding physical ed classes, but when I began Tai Kwon Do, I realized it was more than kicking and punching. It involved self-discipline, meditation, and building self-confidence – all things I needed.

When Ed finished the required course, he quit, but I continued studying with the Master at his studio off-campus. Eventually, I earned my green belt. Forty years later, I surprised my grandson, who was studying Tai Kwon Do, with some of the moves I remembered.

We lived in Sacramento from 1968 to 1970, the height of the hippie, peace, love, and Stop-the-Vietnam War era. Marijuana was readily available. I could almost get high walking across the campus at lunch time. LSD was also available and a certain element thought it was fun to lace Halloween candy with LSD and watch younger children trip. I took Mike and Maureen trick or treating only to close neighbors' and friends' homes. The local firehouse checked Halloween candy for anything unusual.

Since I didn't work outside our home, I had no spending money of my own. Ed's paycheck was budgeted with no funds available for anything but necessities. To earn pocket money to get my hair cut or buy an occasional candy bar, I taught piano lessons to neighborhood children, with limited success. One boy was so angry with his mother for making him take lessons that he tried to set my garage on fire. Years later I found out that he spent his twenties in jail for arson.

Things changed in paradise. It probably began with my increasing need for intellectual stimulation. Ed and the kids were all in school and I was stuck at home. I longed for company and conversation.

I began getting suspicious when Ed started coming home later and later in the evenings, arriving after the kids went to bed. At first, I believed that he was studying on campus with his buddies. But sometimes he'd smell like he had just taken a shower, and other times, I'd get a whiff of a woman's perfume on his clothes. I realized that my husband was having affairs. Any free time he had, whether during the day or in the evening, he would spend with one woman or another and tell me he was in a study group.

Meanwhile, he signed up for a parenting course and for group therapy. Both would keep him out of the house in the evening. Normally, a parenting course would be attended by both parents. Since we couldn't afford the double fee, he took the course while I stayed home actually parenting our two children.

Ed attended a weekend group therapy session at the home of the therapist. It ran from Friday evening to Sunday afternoon. When I arrived to pick him up, he wasn't ready to leave. He was giving a woman a foot massage. That upset me. I would beg him to massage my legs when I was pregnant. I'd had frequent leg cramps from standing on the cement floor. He never massaged my legs.

Sometime after that, I began putting the kids to bed each night then sitting in a tub of the hottest water I could tolerate for hours. I felt I had to punish myself for not being good enough or interesting enough for my husband to spend his time with me. He would come home after midnight, long after I went to bed.

I remember feeling worthless, mechanically going through my everyday chores – taking care of the kids, cooking, cleaning. I gave up trying to converse with Ed. If he asked a question, I would respond. He decided I needed therapy and took me to the therapist's house for the weekend therapy session. I don't remember much from that weekend. I know I cried a lot, talked a lot, and slept a lot. When I got home, I didn't feel as worthless. I returned to my household routine but stopped punishing myself with the hot water. Life continued as if nothing happened. I did continue to see the therapist to work on my self-esteem until we left for our next assignment. Ed and I didn't speak of the affairs though I did talk about them with the therapist.

When Ed graduated with a degree in civil engineering, he was sent to Officer Candidate School in Texas. The kids and I remained in Sacramento. When he completed the school, he was declared 'an officer and a gentleman' by an act of Congress.

His next assignment was in Spokane, Washington. I looked forward to the relocation as a new beginning.

22.

Eastern Washington State 1971–1972

When it appeared that Ed would be stationed in Spokane for a while, I went back to college and majored in journalism. It was an easy decision. I didn't want to be a music teacher and I couldn't make it as a concert pianist. My second love was writing.

Unsure of when we might move again, I crammed my last two years of college into one year. My kids were in first and second grades and my classes were scheduled while they were in school. After school, I did all the household chores, and when the kids went to bed at 9 p.m., so did I. I'd get up at 2 a.m. to study and type my reports with no interruptions.

Ed was away on Air Force missions most of that year. When home, he grumbled that my typing in the middle of the night disturbed his sleep. I set the manual typewriter on a pillow to mute the sound.

In my last trimester, I opted to take an internship rather than the final college courses. I would be more marketable with job experience. Although the college would sanction an internship, I had to find a place that would take me. I made the rounds of newspapers, radio and TV stations. Women were not yet allowed in newsrooms in the 1970s.

Newspapers hired women to write stories for the society page or to write obituaries – no hard news. Radio did not like women's voices reading serious news on the air. TV had just begun to use 'weather girls.' I was lucky to find a progressive television news director who would guide me because he felt I was a good writer and photographer.

Three days before I was to begin the internship though, he died, and the new director didn't want a woman in his newsroom. I had to fight to make him honor the commitment made by his predecessor. At first, he ignored me. Then he decided to use me as his errand person, delivering messages around the building, picking up film at the lab, making coffee. I wasn't learning anything on the seven-to-three shift. In desperation, I appealed to the news director in charge of the three-to-eleven shift.

Sherman was a crusty former newspaper editor and I learned a lot from him. He told me to never give up and to keep fighting for what I wanted. He paired me with a young Native American, Jim, who was an excellent cameraman. Together we filmed and wrote the news stories to be broadcast at 11:00 p.m. We were the odd couple; the rest of the news staff were white males.

In 1973, local news was captured on film, and interviews were conducted and written. Then the film was developed and spliced to fit the stories. Newsmen read the stories on the air while the film was shown.

I remember three of the stories well. The first was an interview with the company that was setting up Expo '74, the World Fair in Spokane, Washington. On our way to the interview, Jim and I were caught in a blinding rainstorm and we arrived dripping wet, although it didn't matter because we were not on camera.

Our next big assignment was a chicken fire: chickens were burning on a farm that supplied the city's supermarkets. We arrived at the scene while the coops were still smoking. The air smelled like burning feathers. We waited until the fire was out before interviewing the owner and the fire chief.

When we got back to the studio, we endured chicken jokes for the rest of our shift. "Hey, where's my order of legs to go?" "You guys smell awful." There was a chicken shortage in Spokane that summer.

Our third memorable assignment began with a notification from the police that a car was stolen and abandoned at a defunct sand pit. Jim filmed the car. The engine was still running and the driver's door was open, the contents of a woman's purse spilled out on the seat. The police searched the nearby woods for signs of the driver, telling us to stay in our van because the man was armed. They found no trace of him.

On our way back to the studio, while we were stopped at a red light, a car backfired. We both ducked. The next sound we heard was a horn. The light was green.

During my three-month stint as a TV newswoman, I appeared in one interview that was filmed in the studio and broadcast. I also did background research and interviews. I wrote the stories which were read on each day's evening news as well as all the station's public service announcements. I even recorded the two-minute sign-off news played at midnight. The station was on the air from 6 a.m. to midnight.

The college charged me tuition for 15 credits and I earned an A for the internship. My pay from the TV station was a one-year subscription to TV Guide magazine.

23.

Spokane – Living the Good Life 1971–1976

Everything about our stay in Spokane was different. Ed was an officer.

This was the first time we lived on a military base. We were assigned a three-bedroom house in a section of the base reserved for officers. Our belongings were unpacked for us. Things would be better as an officer's wife, or so I thought. I was unaware of the social rules I would have to follow.

We were given a guide like the one you get in a hotel, describing the area: the restaurants, churches, movie theaters, lakes, and ski resorts. It also included a list of bars and other venues we were not allowed to visit. Rules for living in base housing were part of the guide. Your family could be evicted for infractions.

The lawn had to be mowed to exactly 1 ½ inches high and had to be watered on a strict schedule. All the walls were painted white – no colors allowed. Pictures could be hung only on existing hooks. Our house was subject to random inspections.

One of the perks of being an officer was the Officer's Club on the base. It had a pool, a bar and a restaurant. On Friday evenings during the summer, Ed and I met our friends there for happy hour, dinner and dancing. Our kids were allowed to use the pool while we were there.

The social obligations of an officer's wife were many –
mandatory membership in the officers' wives' club, attendance
at receptions for visiting dignitaries (formal attire required),
and participation in any charitable event hosted by the high-
ranking officers' wives. The junior officers' wives were
expected to get to know the rest of the women by joining the
golf or bridge club. Since I had no interest in either of those
activities, I sang with the choral group. The wives' club
published a monthly magazine and initially I wrote a few
articles and took photos for it, and then subsequently became
the editor.

Before the magazine could be printed, it had to be approved
by the base commander and all the top-ranking officers' wives.
I was reprimanded before my first issue ever went to press. I
had listed the top officers' wives in alphabetical order rather
than in order of their husbands' rank.

Ed and I were obligated to attend a cocktail hour followed by
dinner at the Officers' Club. The cocktail hour dragged on for
two hours. I was hungry and I knew the kitchen shut down at 8
p.m. I expressed my concern to one of the 'high-ranking'
women. She said, "We have to wait for the general to make the
move." I thought that was ridiculous – he probably didn't know
the time schedule.

I spotted the general speaking with a colonel and waited
politely until he turned to me. "General, you are probably
getting hungry. I know I am, and the kitchen closes in half an
hour." He smiled and said, "Would you do me the honor of
escorting me into the dining room?"

The room fell silent as the general navigated the crowd with
a lowly lieutenant's wife on his arm. Ed followed us. I

introduced him to the general when we got to the table. The general pulled out my chair. The base commander and his wife hurried to join us. The wing commander's wife glared at me while she and her husband looked for another table. Ed and I had taken their place. I was earning a reputation.

We lived on the base for a little over a year. Then we bought a house in town. It was a big, old house with five bedrooms, a Dutch glass brick fireplace, a built-in china cabinet, and a large front porch. The hardwood floors were light with a darker wood pattern around the edges, and there were mahogany railings on the stairway, and two pocket doors. I loved that house.

Although I thought the house was in great shape when we bought it, Ed's dream was to renovate it and create a three-room apartment that we could rent for extra income. The house was under construction almost the entire time we lived there. However, Ed paused the renovation during the summer of 1974.

Expo 74 took place in Spokane. It was called the Environmental World's Fair because it focused on the environment. The city did a great job cleaning up the skid row area and building the expo site. Spokane Falls was a major attraction and it was lit up at night. Visitors could walk across a rope bridge and look down on the falls.

One detail the planners forgot to address – the city had only two major hotels. Many Spokanites rented out rooms in their homes. An enterprising RV dealer set up his inventory in a field and rented the vehicles like motel rooms. Camping was encouraged. So many of our friends visited that year that I felt like a bed and breakfast manager.

During the fair, Mike and Maureen performed with their school music groups on the outdoor stage. I performed with the Spokane Community Chorus accompanied by the Spokane Symphony Orchestra in the newly built Spokane Opera House. We felt like movie stars.

After graduating from Eastern Washington State University, I worked for *United Way* as public relations director. During the Expo, I had to go to the fairgrounds twice a week to collect the coins tossed into a fountain as donations. I showed my ID at the gate and got a free entry pass which was valid all day. After work I'd take the kids to the Expo for free.

On Friday and Saturday nights the fair closed at 10 p.m. with a spectacular fireworks display, and we'd watch it from our second-floor bathroom window.

When the Expo ended, Ed continued his renovation of the house. But before he'd completed it, he received orders for Thailand. The kids and I could not accompany him and he'd be away for a year. I decided to stay in Spokane instead of moving home to Connecticut. Then my job at *United Way* was eliminated.

I finished the painting and redecorating. but unfortunately, I didn't get to enjoy the finished project. When Ed returned from Thailand, we moved to Tacoma.

24.

Peak Experience

Spokane had two seasons – summer and winter. Summers were warm with the temperatures sometimes reaching 100 degrees. The humidity was low so the heat was tolerable and we didn't need an air conditioner in the house.

In the winters, snow began accumulating before Halloween and didn't stop until Mother's Day. Fairchild Air Force Base, where we lived our first winter, was on a hill above the town. Frequently the road would be closed due to blizzard conditions.

The base had a series of anti-fog machines surrounding the runways. The machines sprayed chemicals into the air that made the fog look like it was snowing sideways. The runways had to be kept clear in case of a national emergency. As part of the base civil engineering squadron, Ed oversaw the snowplow brigade.

After we bought the house in town, we had frequent house parties. On Thanksgiving, we hosted 20 people – couples with children, singles, anyone who was far from family. After dinner we settled in to watch *Willy Wonka and the Chocolate Factory.* It was on TV every Thanksgiving.

Invariably, the Air Force would call the squadron out to plow the runways while the rest of us watched the movie. At least the squad members got to eat first.

To survive the winters, friends convinced us to take up skiing. and they took turns teaching all of us. Mike and Maureen were soon plunging down the beginner slopes with no problems. Ed caught on quickly. I fell 15 times on the way to the chair lift. I was miserable, cold, and wet.

The second ski trip was much better. I bought a waterproof ski outfit and as I got comfortable on the mountain I looked forward to skiing.

In 1975, with the money I'd earned working, we bought a condo at Jackass Ski Bowl in northern Idaho. It slept eight so we always had guests on the weekends. The area has been bought, renovated, expanded, and sold a few times. It is now known as Silver Mountain Resort.

We were living the good life – two incomes, lots of entertaining, ski trips. But beneath all the good times, I felt a foreboding, which I ignored. Until Ed went to Thailand.

25.

My 32nd Year – 1975

My marriage reached critical mass in my 32nd year. The excitement of Expo '74 was over, and I was laid off by *United Way* because of budget cuts – or so they said. I knew that wasn't true because the agency had its biggest annual fund-raising campaign ever, thanks to my ideas and publicity. It was paying me the same rate as an entry level secretary because I was a woman, even though I had a college degree. No benefits were included because I was a military wife.

The head of the agency got rid of me because I knew he was having an affair with the bookkeeper. Both were married. Two months after I left, he hired a young man to replace me at double my salary plus benefits.

Ed was working in Thailand for a year, unaccompanied by family, or in his case unencumbered. He set up housekeeping with a Thai woman. He bought her gifts, took her on a safari, and vacationed with her in exclusive hotels. He charged all his expenses to my credit card. I'd given him access for emergencies. His idea of an emergency was that his mistress wanted a diamond bracelet and he didn't have the cash for it. He must have thought that I paid the bills without reading them.

At that time, Mike was ten and Maureen was nine. Although their dad was away, their daily routines continued but with less stress. They didn't have to adjust much because even when he was home, he wasn't with us. I remember two weeks when

Ed went into work before the kids were up and came home after they went to bed. The second Friday they asked if he was coming home for dinner. I told them that he left Thursday for a three-month class in Ohio. They said they didn't notice that he was gone because he wasn't around much anyway.

The summer of 1975 passed uneventfully. Because I wasn't working, the kids and I had a lot of fun. We spent time at a lake with friends. We hiked and picked huckleberries on the mountain in Idaho and stayed at our condominium. The kids learned to fish from one neighbor and to play tennis from another.

In early November, we were driving back home from the condo and got caught in a blizzard. Our normal two-hour drive took four and a half hours. The only way I could drive was in the tracks of the car ahead of me. I had to follow its taillights. A tractor-trailer passed us going in the opposite direction and so much snow was thrown on my windshield that I couldn't see. I slid off the road onto the shoulder. I regained my composure, gripped the steering wheel, and returned to the tracks I had been following. When we finally arrived home, I trembled for half an hour.

Two days later, I received a call from one of the other unit owners. Our building was hit by an avalanche and pushed four feet off its foundation. But it wasn't an avalanche of snow. It was mud that had slid down the mountain. Slowly and steadily, it nudged the building out of its path.

I phoned the other owners, an attorney, and the resort owner. I had to get in touch with Ed in Thailand. I went to the *Red Cross* office for help because I knew the director through my job with the *United Way*. The director asked if I wanted my husband home, because he could arrange a hardship transfer.

Five days later, Ed arrived. He had his suitcase in hand and was wearing an angry look, though I didn't find out why until weeks later. Since he had already served over half his time, he wouldn't be going back to Thailand. He was angry with me for breaking up his living arrangements early. The Air Force shipped all his belongings home, including the love letters from two women which were packed with his dirty laundry.

On his first night back after being away for seven months, he had no loving arms for me. His mistress gave him a gift which required daily doses of penicillin. It was just as well that he went to Idaho for a month to engineer the reconstruction of the condo building. When I found the letters, I knew our marriage wouldn't survive. Nevertheless, when his orders came through for Tacoma, Washington, I prepared for the move.

Two years later I divorced him.

26.

Kitty

A scruffy sliver of grey and white fur wandered onto our porch. It was instant love for Mike and Maureen but not for me. No cat was going to move into my house. I disliked cats, stealthy creatures who'd launch sneak attacks with claws out.

I allowed an occasional saucer of milk on the porch, thinking the novelty would wear off in a few days. A week passed. Every day when I arrived home from work, the kids would be outside playing with the cat. After her evening saucer of milk, the cat disappeared under the porch. Each morning she would appear at the door waiting for the kids to get her breakfast.

A week later, my brother-in-law came to visit. The cat was nowhere in sight when I got home from work and I thought she'd run away. But when I walked into the kitchen, there she was.

"What's that cat doing in here?"

My brother-in-law said, "She looked sick this morning, so I took her to the vet. She must have these pills three times a day for 10 days. You'll have to keep her where you can give her the medicine. See, she's already box trained. I bought enough litter and food to last a month."

"Please, can we keep her, Mom," begged the kids. "We'll take care of her ourselves. We even named her – Kitty."

I lost the cat battle. Kitty grew strong and healthy with an abundance of love and attention. She was aloof from the start, tolerating attention on her terms only.

She disappeared within a month. The kids searched the house and scoured the neighborhood. They were certain that someone had stolen their kitty.

As mysteriously as she vanished, Kitty appeared again a week later in time for breakfast. Perhaps she used the time away to consider her options. There was much weeping and rejoicing by the kids upon Kitty's return and I was also happy to see her.

Kitty decided that she was not our cat, but we were her chosen family. She never left us again. Eventually, we allowed her to roam the neighborhood during the day. She always came back in time for supper.

In the two years she lived with us, I learned to love and respect Kitty's aloofness. She in turn respected my privacy. She sat in my lap and allowed me to pet her when she sensed I was in need. When I felt overwhelmed or depressed, she rubbed against my legs and purred to soothe me. I had conversations with her about my feelings of inadequacy and depression. She looked at me with her big green eyes and I felt understood.

When Kitty went in heat for the first time, it was a nightmare for all of us. She screamed night and day for nearly a week. The next time, I let her satisfy her instinct.

The evening before she gave birth, I could tell her time was near. Kitty lay on the carpet while I stroked her bulging belly, the only time she allowed that during her pregnancy. Then she disappeared in the basement.

Two days later, Kitty came upstairs looking for food. Her belly was gone. She was hungry. The kids tried to follow her to her hiding place, but she slipped away.

A week passed with Kitty eating in the kitchen twice a day then disappearing back into the basement. After breakfast one day, she returned to meow at the kitchen door. I opened it and she deposited a ball of orange and white fluff at my feet. Its eyes were barely open. It was complaining loudly for its size.

Kitty brought her kitten to the center of the kitchen for all to admire while she circled it purring. We weren't allowed to touch it or get too close. A few days later, I found another kitten in the ruffled covers of Maureen's bed.

I had prepared a box for Kitty before the kittens were born. I set the box on the floor and put the kitten in it. Kitty meowed her objection and started to remove her kitten to take it back to the basement. I managed to stop her before she reached the stairs.

"Look," I said. "Can we talk this over?"

She put the kitten back in the box.

There were five kittens in all – two males and three females. We found homes for two of them, one ran away, and one was killed by a dog. We kept the remaining kitten, a striped female, and named her Tigger. I took Kitty to the vet to have her spayed. I told her about it first. She understood and went calmly when the time came.

Ed had been away for six months. When he came back, he was distant, cold. Kitty sensed it and avoided him.

I was sick for a few days and not able to clean the litter box or get the kids to do it. Kitty and Tigger were using the basement floor. Ed raged when he discovered the mess and decided the cats had to go. He grabbed Tigger and stuffed her in a laundry bag. Kitty knew what he was going to do so she hid. No amount of bribery or sweetness on his part would coax her out. He finally gave up and went out for a drive. As soon as he left, Kitty emerged from the basement.

Then Kitty and I had our final talk. She purred softly while I petted her for what would be the last time. She knew her fate and accepted it calmly. I cried while stroking her, trying to gain strength from her calm.

"I think he's getting rid of me too," I sobbed into her fur. "At least you'll be spared the pain."

The door opened. Ed came in. Kitty stopped purring.

27.

The Tacoma Aroma – 1976

Leaving Spokane was bittersweet. Ed had gone ahead to Tacoma while the kids and I stayed until the end of the school year. The move would provide me with the opportunity to start over again – again. This time I insisted on marriage counselling.

Ed attended marriage counselling with me when he was around if only to shut me up. As usual, he would get sent on temporary duty to other bases across the country. These trips lasted from a week to three months. I continued to go to counselling while he was gone. I still had poor self-esteem despite having earned a college degree.

Despite being in counselling, I fell into a depression. I felt useless – no job, no friends, no connections. Mike and Maureen were growing up and didn't need me as much. I had no purpose. I hadn't felt like that since Sacramento. The kids would get home from school and find me asleep on the couch in the dark.

"Are you sick again, Mom?"

"No, I'm just tired."

No matter how I felt, my presence was expected at the Officers' Club social events. My duty was to stand by my man. I put on my happy face and chatted with Ed's squadron commander and his wife, who lived in the house behind ours. Their teenage son had taken up photography. He had a darkroom set up in their basement. The parents invited me to use it. Finally, I found a purpose. I could hone the skills I learned in college. Until rumors spread that I was sneaking out at night to have sex with Ed's commanding officer while Ed was away. The truth was the family was usually out in the evening. I worked in their basement which had an outside entrance.

Then we had a visitor – an old girlfriend of Ed's from Sacramento who was "passing through" and needed a place to stay. We had a sofa bed. He snuck out of our bed and went to sleep with her in the living room.

In the morning I confronted him.

"I want her out of my house now."

"But where will she stay?"

"I don't care. Get her out now."

The next day I went to see the counsellor.

"I want this marriage to work."

"Stop being a martyr," he said. "This is not a marriage."

I quit the sessions.

Months later, I went to see him again. "I'm getting a divorce."

"I knew you would when you got strong enough."

When we fought, Ed threatened me with divorce knowing that scared me because we were Catholic. "If I ever tell you that I want a divorce, I will say it one time and mean it," I said. And that's the way it happened.

I was driving back from our condo in Idaho in the dark and the rain because Ed was too tired. I had cleaned the place and packed for the trip home while he napped. It was my birthday, and he didn't even acknowledge it. The kids were asleep in the back seat. I looked over at him sleeping. Something inside me snapped. With tears running down my cheeks I thought, 'I'm going to divorce you.'

When we got back home, I told him I was going to leave him. He laughed, "You'll never get along without me."

Within a few weeks, I found a job and rented a house. With the help of friends with pick-up trucks, I moved off the base and out of his life.

My job was in Tacoma and the house was in the suburbs. There was a smelter in the industrial part of the city where iron metal was produced from its ore. On days when the wind blew toward the suburbs, the odor from the smelter would gag a maggot. It made my eyes burn. It smelled like rotten eggs, garbage, and burning plastic. The locals called it the "Tacoma aroma."

The 'aroma' was a reminder that at this point my life stank.

28.

Life Change

I walked out of the courtroom a free woman. Funny, I didn't feel free. In fact, I felt nothing at all. I was numb. With a few legal words, my 15-year marriage was over.

"My marriage is irretrievably broken," I read to the judge from my index cards. This was Washington, a community property state, where do-it-yourself divorce was allowed in 1978. Very civilized. No lawyers to muck things up. No prolonged court battles over child custody, possessions, or bills. Just four typed sheets dividing everything we owned. I got custody of Mike and Maureen, the furniture, and half the bills. Ed got custody of four houses, a condo, and half the bills. The marriage was 'irretrievably broken,' unable to be repaired, unsalvageable. Lord knows, I tried. Counseling, crying, praying, pleading, all for nothing. Until that's what I felt: nothing. Zilch. No pain or tears, just a mind-numbing calm. When I was angry, I felt something. I had some passion. But now I stepped off the edge of a deep abyss into a black nothing, no anger or sorrow, certainly no joy.

I was able to function basically. Get up, get the kids to school, go to work, cook, do the laundry. At night, I'd crawl back under the covers into nothing. I wanted to go home to my family in Connecticut but I didn't have the money. I took a second job on weekends and saved all I could for a year – my year of numbness. Then it was time. I picked the first of August to leave Washington and head back to Connecticut. The kids would start high school in September. I gave notice at my jobs and began packing.

I reserved a U-Haul truck and planned to drive it and tow my station wagon. One teensy problem: I couldn't reach the pedals in the truck. No one in my family was willing or able to help. I placed ads for a driver in the local newspaper and on supermarket and church bulletin boards. I'd pay the driver's air fare back to Tacoma and provide meals along the way. Two weeks to go and I still had no truck driver.

When I got into my car to go to work the next morning, it wouldn't start. Finally, I felt something. It was rage. I shook my fists skyward and got mad at God. "What do you expect me to do now?" I sobbed. I called my gas station and asked for help. The serviceman said they were busy, but he thought the owner might be available. And he was. His name was Jerry. I knew all the attendants, but I hadn't met the owner. When I bought gas, Jerry was usually in the office doing owner stuff. Jerry picked me up in a truck, towed my car to the station, and took me to work.

When he drove me home, he noticed all the boxes in my house and asked if I were going somewhere. I told him the story, leaving out the sobbing part. He asked for my phone number; he had an idea and would call me later.

"I'll do it on one condition," Jerry said, " that you let me bring my sons Tracy and Tom with me. None of us has ever been to the east coast." We had a deal. He would drive the truck, I'd drive my car, and Tracy would fill in if one of us got tired. Tracy could reach the pedals in the truck. Jerry was responsible for all the expenses for his sons. I'd pay for Jerry's food, all the gas for both vehicles, and for his plane ticket back.

We headed east on August 1, 1979. It took 10 days for the crossing. My life was irretrievably changed.

Part IV

Second Marriage & Loss

29.

The Long Trip Home – 1979

Our trip from Tacoma to Connecticut was a large undertaking. We were an odd caravan: two adults, four teenagers, and a cat, in a U-Haul truck with attached trailer followed by a station wagon. I didn't know anything about Jerry or his sons. I was desperate, I had to trust him. We were on a 3000-mile road trip during a nationwide gas shortage. Besides, any guy who brought his kids with him seemed okay.

We began our journey with a roast beef lunch at Jerry's mother's house midway across Washington. She cooked a huge meal with enough meat for sandwiches to get us through the next day.

It was a short drive through the Idaho panhandle. But it seemed like it took forever to cross Montana. We feared running out of gas in the middle of nowhere. There's a lot of nowhere in the center of nothing in Montana. We had two five-gallon gas cans with us just in case.

There were no cell phones then. We had walkie talkies to communicate between the truck and the car. Tracy was driving when the car had a blowout. We pulled over and waited for him to catch up. Exits and gas stations were miles apart and we needed to have the tire repaired. Fortunately, the next one wasn't far. It was a very hot day. We used the facilities and lined up to get a cold soda from a machine while we waited. The machine was broken and the soda was warm. So were we. Tempers flared.

When the tire was fixed, we drove east on the highway until we spotted a river paralleling the road. We pulled over. All of us jumped into the river with our clothes on. Though the water was warm, it was refreshing. We sat in the shade and dried off before getting back into the vehicles. That night, still in Montana, we stayed in a motel, took real showers, and slept in real beds. The next morning, everyone was feeling better.

We drove south to Wyoming to detour through Yellowstone National Park so that Jerry and the boys could see the sights – Old Faithful, El Capitan, Bridal Veil Falls. Jerry was edgy driving through the mountains on narrow winding roads. I was appalled when he retrieved a pint bottle of vodka from the glove compartment, took a swig and offered me one. We had an argument. I told him he couldn't drink and drive. He got so angry he threw the bottle out the window and it smashed on the pavement. We didn't speak until we stopped for the night. Tracy saw the bottle fly out the window and asked me what happened. He said his father drank a lot but was never mean or abusive. To his credit, Jerry didn't have another drink until we got to Connecticut and the trip was over.

Although there were only six of us, we spent the night in Ten Sleep, Wyoming. It had been an Indian rest stop so named because it was ten sleeps or ten days travel from Yellowstone. We slept in the truck and station wagon with the windows open. We didn't see any bugs but at daybreak, we woke up slapping ourselves. We'd been breakfast for the no-see-'ems!

We drove onward to Devil's Tower National Monument. We saw it from miles away – it's over 1000 feet high. We pulled into an empty field to eat our picnic lunch – at least, we thought it was empty. There were curious mounds on the terrain, and prairie dogs began popping up out of them, stretching as far as we could see. It looked like a giant Whack-a-Mole and the animals were our lunch entertainment.

We followed Interstate 90, which brought us through the Black Hills of South Dakota and our next tourist stop, Mount Rushmore. The educational value was lost on the boys. They were excited about buying T-shirts emblazoned with *We're somewhere behind Mount Rushmore* over a photo of four giant naked men bending over the mountain.

We made it through Minnesota to Madison, Wisconsin, arriving after midnight. Again, we slept in the vehicles. We were low on gas and parked at the pumps in a gas station so we'd be first in line when it opened. There were no bugs. I guess the smell of the gas kept them away.

I knew that a friend who had been stationed with us in Spokane was now living in Madison and we met him for breakfast. He was so happy to see Mike, Maureen and me that he lifted all three of us off the ground in a group hug. He was big and tall. He called us the little O'Reillys.

The remainder of the trip seemed like one continuous big city. We skirted around Chicago to avoid some of the traffic. Getting back on I-90, we crossed through the top of Indiana into Ohio. And there we had a problem. The trailer hitch came apart. Jerry tied it with a rope and we found a U-Haul place to get it repaired. After working on it for an hour, the mechanic gave up. We had to get a different trailer. We unloaded the contents of the trailer – bicycles, lawnmower, gas cans, leftovers that didn't fit in the truck. I was tempted to leave it behind. All the major furniture and appliances were in the truck. However, the bikes were the last gift Ed bought the kids – I had to take them. After loading everything into a new trailer, we were exhausted. Our one day in Cleveland felt like a week.

We got a motel on the Pennsylvania border, and from there, it was a short drive to our next stop, Niagara Falls. We spent the whole day sightseeing and rented rooms in a motel from where we could see the nightly light show on the falls. It was spectacular.

Our trip was over. We arrived at my sister's house and unloaded everything into her garage. The kids, the cat and I lived in her unfinished attic, where we slept on our mattresses on the floor. Living there was a strain on all of us. My sister and her husband had two boys – a 6-month-old and a 4-year-old. And they had a dog. The hardest challenge was keeping the dog from hunting the cat. I bought a gate to block the stairs. Occasionally, the cat came halfway down the stairs to taunt the dog.

There would be much barking, hissing, meowing and yelling. My sister and her husband would yell at me and my kids.

"Get that cat upstairs!"

"Be quiet, you'll wake the baby!"

And the ever popular, "Do you have to stomp up the stairs?"

The teenagers replied inaudibly, "Yes, because we don't have a door to slam." When they brought the cat back upstairs, I swear it was smirking.

I was highly motivated to find a job and an apartment of my own. Within a month, we settled into our own place. The cat was content with her freedom restored. She could now roam outdoors like she used to out west and she brought us thank you gifts in appreciation.

We unpacked our belongings and settled in our apartment. We were finally home.

30.

Bones of Contention

When I got married and left home, I didn't look back. I didn't feel homesick. I was excited to begin my own life. Perhaps that's why, when I moved back to Connecticut 15 years later, I didn't fit in. Especially with my siblings. They both had spouses, and by then I was a single parent. They lived in a coupled society and I was struggling to survive.

In 1979, my parents were still alive, as was my grandmother, and I wanted my children to get to know them. Since Ed and I were from the same town, there were relatives from his family to get to know as well. To this day, I have relationships with many of the nieces and nephews from Ed's family but no close contact with either my sister or my brother or their families. I have many cousins who are close to me and a few who are not.

In the years I lived away, communication was limited. Ed and I didn't have a telephone until we lived in Oregon. Even then, we used it sparingly because it was expensive for long distance calls. The main way to engage with my family was by letter. My parents wrote occasionally. My grandmother sent birthday cards and Christmas cards. My sister sent postcards from her vacations. My brother never wrote.

My hopes of having a friendship with my siblings never materialized. When my parents were alive, the family celebrated holidays at my sister's house. Though I offered to host, they never came to my house because they had always gathered at my sister's house and that wasn't going to change.

I moved home to be with family, but I was still alone.

Sister Sue, brother Jack, Mom & Dad, June 11, 1986,
my parents' 45th wedding anniversary

31.

My Career Was Looking for a Job

When you are a child, adults ask you, "What do you want to be when you grow up?" My answers were not acceptable – happy, successful, a wife and mother, loved. I was expected to say a specific career like teacher, nurse, secretary.

My mother's dream of being a music teacher never materialized. She became a nurse because it was a profession that paid a salary while you learned. Ma instilled her dream in me. When asked, I'd respond, "I want to be a music teacher." I never explored any other possibilities.

After two years majoring in music, I quit college, married and had two kids. When I had a chance to go back to school several years later, I chose to get my degree in Journalism because I enjoyed writing. After graduation, there were several jobs with non-profit organizations including the March of Dimes, the Red Cross and the American Cancer Society. Jobs with nonprofits are rewarding emotionally but not monetarily.

My favorite job was with the March of Dimes in Tacoma, Washington. There were two paid employees – the executive director and me. My position included secretarial duties, publicity, assisting the director with bookkeeping, and recruiting and supervising volunteers.

The March of Dimes ran three major fundraisers a year – a Mothers' March against birth defects, a Walk-a-thon, and a Haunted House for which we solicited high school clubs for volunteers. Each club – Future Teachers, Spanish – populated a room with ghosts and goblins to scare visitors. There was stiff competition among the actors.

The director at the March of Dimes in Tacoma was the best boss I had. She clearly valued me. In turn I worked my hardest and enjoyed every minute, even when stuffing envelopes or controlling the crowd during a Walk-a-thon in the rain.

I regretted leaving the March of Dimes to move back home to Connecticut. The "Land of Steady Habits" did not take kindly to a single mom from the west coast. Obtaining a job in Connecticut was more difficult than in Washington. It was hard to get an interview unless you had a connection and I had no connections. I had been away too long. The few interviewers I spoke with dismissed me because I was overqualified and I had a west coast attitude. Translation: my college degree threatened them and I was too friendly. I didn't share their Nutmegger aloofness.

For a while, I worked for a temp agency. The assignments lasted from one week to three months and never converted to a permanent job.

I scoured the want ads and bulletin boards. I registered with job agencies. I mailed resumes. I talked to everyone I knew. My permanent job was looking for a job. I existed on unemployment payments from Washington and shopped for food in my mother's freezer. The kids and I didn't have a pasta night – it was rare to have a meal that *wasn't* pasta. My kids helped out by getting jobs after school in a greenhouse planting vegetables and flowers.

When Maureen told one of her teachers I was looking for a job, the teacher referred me to the Red Cross, and I was hired. At the same time, I got a part-time job as a waitress at Denny's.

Between the two I made enough money to pay rent and buy food.

After working from 8 a.m. to 4:30 p.m. at the Red Cross, I'd change into my Denny's uniform and work six more hours. I had no days off. I worked 76 hours a week. In my spare time, I looked for a better job that paid enough that I wouldn't have to work two jobs.

Each time I changed jobs it was for a few more dollars, until I landed a job with the State of Connecticut. To qualify, I had to submit proof that I had a college degree and take an exam like the SAT. At the time I was working in public relations at a college. I took a pay cut to get into the state system but I made it up in a few years. And the benefits were excellent.

Even while working for the state, I kept looking for a better paying job. I applied for every open position that was announced if it meant a pay raise. I took all the state-run classes to gain more skills. I took the GRE and enrolled in college to get a master's degree. After completing three courses I realized that the advanced degree would not be an advantage in a job search. I would again be over-qualified.

I spent 16 years working for the state. Although there were some trying times – furloughs, increased workload but static salary, demotion due to budget cuts – I retired with excellent health care and a pension. For a few years after I retired, I still scoured the want ads for that perfect career. It was a lifelong habit.

32.

How We Met – 1995

For 17 years after my divorce, I hung out in bars, joined singles clubs and dating services, and answered newspaper ads, attempting to meet eligible men. Those I met fell into three categories: married, alcoholic, or both. Another group of single men hung out at my house. They were my son's friends – not dating material. I finally gave up. My son and daughter were grown and had lives of their own. Companionship would have been nice, but I was comfortable by myself and I had a good job.

The men I worked with fell into the same categories: married, alcoholic or 'no-way-I'm-old-enough-to-be-your-mother.' One of the married men, who I thought was rude and crude, cornered me in the elevator. Lennie Slitt was 6 feet and over 200 pounds. I'm vertically challenged at 4 feet 11.5 inches, and I weigh . . . never mind what I weigh. I am not overweight - I'm under-tall.

The elevator door was almost shut when someone did a hand swipe to open it. Oh, no, I shuddered. It's that crude Lennie guy. He pushed the *close* button and gave me a Cheshire Cat grin.

"This is your lucky day," he said. "Bet you wish you could go out with me."

"Maybe, if you were the last man on earth," I said. Fortunately, I didn't run into him alone again. I started taking the stairs.

When I joined the office bowling team, I found out that Mr. Rude and Crude was also loud and obnoxious. Lennie was the team captain, and I was afraid of him. When he missed a spare, he'd yell some not-so-nice words and kick the return carousel. He threw the ball with such force that the pins exploded. When I threw the ball, it would nudge the pins over, if it didn't land in the gutter.

One morning, I heard Lennie telling a co-worker that he had gotten a divorce.

"I'm sorry," I said.

"I'm not," he said.

A year later, I posted a cartoon on the bulletin board. I don't even remember what it was. I received a message on my computer from Mr. Rude and Crude.

"Did you post that cartoon?" I felt safe answering because he worked in another part of the building.

"Yes, so?"

"You're such a women's libber."

I didn't respond.

"Why haven't you asked me out?"

I was shocked! Here was a man I had no interest in, flirting with me.

"I don't ask men out. I'm old fashioned that way."

A very long pause followed. Then, "If I asked you out, would you go out with me?"

Wow, his bravado was not what I expected. "I don't know, you'll have to ask me to find out."

An even longer pause. Then on screen, "Would yoo gout with mee?" My first inclination was to correct his typos, but I resisted. I was curious. What's the worst that could happen? I'd get a free meal, he'd find out we had nothing in common, and he'd go away and leave me alone.

"Yes."

Turns out that was absolutely the right answer. I did get a free meal and a single rose. Who knew? The guy was a romantic. The rude and obnoxious persona only existed at work. We had a lot in common. I had a wonderful evening.

After we got married, Lennie looked at me and said, "I didn't know that being the last man on earth would make me so happy!"

33.

Catholic Guilt

Lennie and I were raised similarly though I was Catholic and he was Jewish. One of the drawbacks of growing up Catholic in the 1950s was the generous amount of guilt you were served. That was also true for Jewish children.

I felt guilty whenever anything went wrong. Children were starving in China – my fault. My siblings were fighting – my fault. The kitchen sink leaked – my fault.

I was a 'good girl.' I obeyed my parents and teachers. I obeyed the Ten Commandments – no lying, cheating, or stealing. Once a month, all students were taken to the church next door for confession. My sin was making up sins. I had nothing to confess. I would say, "I lied three times since my last confession." The lies I was confessing were the ones I told in my last confession.

My faith in the Church and the nuns and priests teaching me was shaken for the first time by my sixth-grade teacher. She explained the vows of poverty and chastity that she took to become a nun. She told the class that nuns had no worldly possessions. They were given two habits to wear – one for summer and one for winter. They washed them by hand and mended them when needed. I knew this wasn't true. My father was a drycleaner. Once a week he dry-cleaned all the nuns' habits for free. I didn't say anything about my teacher's lie. I wonder if she confessed it.

The second time I was disillusioned was in my senior year of high school. One of my classmates got pregnant – a mortal sin. She was expelled. As yearbook editor, I was directed to remove her photo and any mention of her. Her boyfriend had graduated the previous year. They were forced to marry. They had nothing. Her classmates gave her a bridal shower and provided the linens and household items she needed.

I was called into the principal's office and reprimanded for attending the shower. The nun said I was condoning sin. This time I spoke up. "I thought we were supposed to be charitable and help the needy," I said. "She needs help." I left the room crying.

My third disillusionment happened on a trip to Rome that I took with Ed. We had a chance to see Pope Paul VI in St. Peter's Basilica. The Pope addressed the audience in several languages. The crowd pushed and shoved its way toward the altar to get a better view of the Pope. Bodies were moving like waves in a sea and it was hot. A woman fainted and fell out of sight. Ed pushed his way to her, picked her up and got her to the side of the current of people so she wouldn't be trampled to death. No one else noticed as the crowd surged toward the altar to kiss the pope's ring. I managed to get my back against a wall so I wouldn't be swept away. I clung to the wall for nearly an hour before Ed and I were reunited.

I was in awe of the riches in the basilica – the Pope's gilded chair, the paintings, the sculptures, especially Michelangelo's Pieta. Bejeweled vestments, gold chalices, and other gold vessels were on display in the Vatican Treasury Museum. The poverty of the people outside the entrance to the Vatican was in sharp contrast to the riches within.

At times during my life, I was a devout Catholic attending daily Mass. At other times, I would attend Mass only twice a year – Christmas and Easter. When I got divorced, the priest at my church encouraged me to get an annulment so that I could remain a Catholic in good standing. I was, until I married Lennie, then I was automatically excommunicated. We were both divorced. We eloped and got married by a Justice of the Peace in Vermont. The Catholic church does not recognize civil unions. We were living in sin.

Eventually, I stopped attending Mass. I have problems with Catholicism. I am pro women's rights and gay marriage, horrified by the pedophiles among priests, and by pro-lifers threatening Planned Parenthood clients with guns.

I have no use for hypocritical organized religion. My relationship with my maker is personal. I can pray anywhere. I do not have to be in a gilded building.

34.

She's Back

It was strange waving good bye to my body lying still in the emergency room. I could see the medical team working frantically while I watched them from the ceiling. An out-of-body experience? I had a nagging thought that I must get back. I'm not done yet. I have work to do, grandchildren to see, children who need me. Lennie needs me. We're getting married. As good as I feel now, I can't give up. I have to go back to the pain. I'm not dead yet.

The next thing I remembered was the medic's face close to mine. He was talking loudly. "What's your name? Tell me your name."

I held up my hand with the ID bracelet. "Can't you read?"

"Sheee's baaack," he said.

I felt a collective sigh of relief from the room. When I read my medical records months later, I learned that I had flat-lined for 30 seconds. I had a 99% blockage in one artery. The next day they opened the artery with balloon angioplasty. Now I tell people that my broken heart was repaired on Valentine's Day, February 14, 1997.

35.

Christmas Letter – 1997

Dear Friends:

We had an eventful year including some major life changes beginning last Christmas when Lennie asked me to marry him – I accepted.

* On February 13, I had a major heart attack. Must have been the shock of being engaged after all these years alone. The next day I had an angiogram and angioplasty to remove the 99% blockage in my artery. What better day to have a broken heart fixed but on Valentine's Day?

* The next two months I recuperated at home while Lennie took care of me. Since there was no warning before the heart attack, it appeared that the cause was job stress. I returned to work in April after completing cardiac rehab.

* On May 30, we eloped to Vermont and were married in an historic inn by the innkeeper. It was very romantic.

* Lennie's daughter Becky graduated from Yale in June and remained at Yale to work toward a master's degree.

* On June 6, I began working for the Office of Consumer Counsel, another state agency, doing public relations work. No more Public Utility Control customer service complaints.

* Lennie retired July 1 after working for the state for 32 years.

* We vacationed in Washington state in August, visiting with my daughter Maureen and her family. We also visited with friends, drove around the Olympic peninsula, through the rain forest, and ferried to Victoria, British Columbia, Canada.

* This fall we went leaf peeping in Vermont and New Hampshire. We also drove to Pennsylvania for some sight-seeing and outlet shopping in the heart of Amish country.

* Thanksgiving was shared with Mike, my sister and her family, and Lennie's mother, who turned 80 in November. We celebrated her birthday with Lennie's brother and his family.

* This month I sang with the Masterworks Chorale – still singing after all these years. My long black skirt is older than half of the chorus members! We're busy celebrating both Hanukkah and Christmas together.

We wish you and yours a happy holiday season filled with love.

Judy and Lennie

Lennie and I eloped. Notice the ladder.

36.

Life, Love and Lennie

Our differences were many, but they didn't matter. Lennie and I were in our 50s when we started dating, both set in our ways. We were beyond establishing careers, building a house, raising a family.

Lennie lived in an apartment. He moved in with me and we split the household bills and the chores. The hardest thing for me to adjust to was sharing my space. I had lived alone for 17 years, answering to no one. I had to learn to let Lennie know if I decided to go shopping after work or stop for a drink with a friend.

Lennie's adjustment was harder – he had to give up smoking. And he did – cold turkey – before he moved in with me.

We lived well. With both of us working, we had the means to travel, dine out often, purchase items that we wanted and not just needed. Lennie hadn't travelled much. The first purchase we made together was a set of luggage for him. We took our first trip to Washington state to meet my daughter and her family. Lennie said he couldn't believe he was dating somebody's grandmother. He loved kids. If we lived closer, he would have spoiled them.

While we were visiting, I showed him some of the sights. He'd never been to the west coast. Driving back from Mt. Saint Helens, he said, "For our next vacation, I'd like to go to . . ." and he listed places he would like to see. Every year we made a few trips around the US and Europe.

We enjoyed each other's company. We spent evenings together watching TV or reading. Lennie was an avid reader. When he moved in with his books, we had to buy more shelves. (When he died, I donated 800 books to the public library.) We owned 17 five-shelf bookcases and they were full.

In the time we spent together, Lennie and I had only one serious argument. We were on an Alaskan cruise in September 1999. I needed a band-aid. Lennie told me to get one from his ditty bag. I found a pack of cigarettes and when I confronted him, he admitted to having fallen off the wagon. I felt he should have let me know he was having problems. He didn't want me to think he was weak. My Irish temper kicked in. "So, you'd rather I think you're a liar?" We discussed a reasonable course of action to take when we got home – he would go to the doctor for help. Meanwhile, I wouldn't nag him. We didn't go to bed angry.

Our marriage wasn't perfect. We experienced the everyday bumps that people do when living together. Lennie was a precisionist. That probably came from his accounting background. I was more of a free spirit – an artist.

Lennie made his own lunch at night to take to work the following day. He always made the same lunch – two cold cut sandwiches, a dill pickle, an apple, and a thermos of coffee. I usually looked in the fridge in the morning to see if there were any leftovers I could take. If not, I'd buy my lunch. One morning I made a sandwich and took a pickle. That night when Lennie was making his lunch, he asked me if I took a pickle. I asked, "Why, do you have them numbered?"

We didn't try to change who we were. Some of each of our best traits rubbed off on the other. I became more outspoken and organized. He became more flexible and less angry. He retired five years before I did. He called me at work on a Thursday.

"Tell your boss you have to take Monday off."

"Why? Is something wrong?"

"No, I'll tell you when you get home."

He wanted to prove to me that he could be spontaneous. He said he was taking me shopping for the weekend – to the Mall of America in Minneapolis. He enjoyed surprising me.

37.

Adventures in Ireland – 1999

O, Ireland! isn't it grand you look
Like a bride in her rich adornin!
With all the pent-up love of my heart
I bid you the top of the morning!
The Exiles Return or *Morning on the Irish Coast* by John Locke

It's an overnight flight to Ireland. At the first glimpse of the Emerald Isle in the morning light, this poem always comes to my mind.

The many shades of green glisten in the morning dew. The ever-present rain is counteracted by the friendliness of the Irish. Being the home of Guinness may contribute to their happiness.

It was my second trip to Ireland – this time accompanied by Lennie and Mike. Our tour guide gave us our itinerary and instructions for the next morning.

"The bus will be leaving at nine, so be sure to eat your breakfast early. And if ye not be there by nine, then we'll be leaving by nine turdy." This was Irish time – tardiness was as normal as the rain.

Our guide would announce each morning, "Tis a bit of a soft day." That meant you wouldn't need an umbrella, but you better wear a raincoat.

Dinner at Bunratty Castle

We travelled from the Cliffs of Moher in the west to Dublin in the east, stopping in the towns of Ennis, Galway and Kildare.

We also toured Glendalough, a sixth century monastic settlement. St. Kevin, the patron saint of Dublin and Glendalough, was its founder and first abbot. Many of the ancient buildings still stand, including the chapel. St. Kevin himself supposedly slept in the room above it.

Lennie fell in love with Bewley's Irish coffee and he was determined to bring some home. It wasn't sold in the stores –

only served in restaurants – and he asked the waiter if he could purchase a pound. The waiter gave him a case – 24 one-pound bags. We had to stuff the individual bags in our suitcases, between our clothes, and in our shoes. Our laundry smelled like freshly brewed coffee.

Our group of 30 filled the village pubs where we stopped for lunch. Entertainment was plentiful and free in the pubs. Patrons brought their instruments, including spoons and harmonicas, and joined the house band to make music. Those members of the audience who didn't play an instrument joined in by singing and dancing. A highlight for Mike was playing the fiddle with the house band at one of the pubs.

We visited Newgrange, the 5,000-year-old burial chamber entered through a long stone passage. The entire site is covered by a mound of 200,000 pounds of stone and earth over an acre of land. A small opening over the entryway is a curious feature. Every dawn around the winter solstice, a shaft of sunlight penetrates the opening into the otherwise dark passageway and creeps slowly to the back of the burial chamber, illuminating the drawings on the wall. There is a waiting list of ten years to experience this phenomenon. We settled for a simulation.

I lost Lennie when I went into the gift shop at Newgrange. He was ready to leave and boarded the bus just as the driver headed out to get some coffee. When everyone was on the bus, the driver took a head count; one was missing – Mike. "You'll have to excuse my son – he's Irish," I said. "And forgive my husband, he isn't!"

"Ah, ye poor woman."

38.

The Great Turkey Fryer Fire

Lennie and I flew to Florida in March of 2001 for a vacation and to visit his relatives. We attended a Thanksgiving-like celebration at his cousin's house in Boca Ratan and were served fried turkey. It seems that southerners fry everything: chicken, okra, grits, greens, even Twinkies.

The turkey was delicious – not at all what I expected. It was not greasy but moist and tasty and cooked in a couple of hours. Lennie loved it and so I bought him a fryer when we got home. We used it twice that summer and planned on frying our Thanksgiving turkey.

On Thanksgiving Day, Lennie put the fryer in the backyard far away from the deck and filled it with oil. He turned it on to heat up the oil while he went to get his mother. He told Becky – his daughter – and me to keep an eye on it since we weren't comfortable with it yet. When it reached frying temperature, it was supposed to shut off.

I was about to go out the patio door to check it when I noticed white smoke pouring out the top of it. It hadn't been smoking a minute ago. I called to Becky to look.

Then there was a loud KABOOM! Flames shot up from the fryer. The patio door was suddenly too hot to touch. The deck railing was on fire. I couldn't move. Heat radiated through the glass. Becky grabbed me and headed for the front door while calling 911.

As we got outside, men started arriving in pick-up trucks, shouting, "Where's the fire?" The volunteer fire fighters had arrived – 17 of them – and we led them to the back of the building. They sprayed everything with fire extinguishers and the fire was contained.

Then the full troops arrived – uniformed firemen. The front of the deck railing was crispy, the plastic siding was melted all the way up to the second floor, the fryer was charred, its hose to the propane tank had burned through and was trailing on the ground, and the grass surrounding the tank was black. The fire chief said the fryer was not UL certified. It was supposed to shut off when a specific temperature was reached and it had failed.

Dinner was ruined. We still celebrated with all the side dishes – mashed potatoes, candied yams, cranberry sauce, stuffing, green beans and pumpkin pie. I was thankful we were together, and that the house didn't burn down. It was a turkey-less Thanksgiving.

I was embarrassed because I was president of the condo owners association and my condo unit had caught on fire. I arranged for the fire marshal to give a talk on fire safety to our members at the next general meeting.

The condo association added a rule to the bylaws banning the use of turkey fryers on the property. I've lived here over 30 years. Some of my neighbors still call me Torch.

39.

Parisian Humor

I took Lennie to Paris in October 2001. His friends had told him the French have no sense of humor but he would eventually draw his own conclusions.

We visited the Eiffel Tower one day but only got to go halfway up. I wished Lennie could have experienced the Tower from the top and at night to fully appreciate its grandeur as I had on a previous trip. While the view in the sunshine is spectacular, the view at night is awesome. Paris is called the City of Lights and when seen from the top of the Eiffel Tower at night, you understand why. The avenues are arranged like spokes on a wheel and fan out from the tower in all directions. They are easy to distinguish because they're much broader than the streets.

We skipped dinner with our tour group and headed off on our own so that Lennie could experience the Paris lights. On our way to catch a bus to the Tower, we passed an open butcher shop. I always carry my camera with me in case I come across anything interesting. Skinned rabbits were hanging by their hind legs in a row behind the counter.

"I have to get a picture of this."

"Yeah, yeah, hurry up," Lennie said. He didn't like stopping for my photo ops.

The butcher moved to the far end of the counter to get out of my way. I was taking my time to check the light and focus when one of the rabbits reared up so I could see its face. I let out a squeak and jumped back in surprise. The butcher and Lennie were laughing. Good thing I got the picture before the rabbit moved because it took 15 minutes for my heart to stop thumping.

When we arrived at the Eiffel Tower, a breeze was blowing and it was warm and pleasant. By the time we got to the top, the wind felt like a gale force and when we tried to make our way from the elevator across the viewing platform, the wind kicked up and blew us sideways into the handrail. Fortunately, we were able to work our way around the outside holding on tight to the rail.

Of course, I had to take Lennie's picture although it was difficult to do one-handed; I wasn't going to let go of the railing for anything. I have the photo somewhere – his smile looks more like a grimace and his hair is blown straight up. We were chastised for missing the group dinner, but it was worth it.

On a free afternoon, we went to the largest department store in Paris, the *Samartine*. Each floor of the seven-story building was a different experience, from furs, expensive clothes, and fine jewelry, to gourmet foods and kitchen gadgets. No cheap souvenirs in sight. The center of the building was open with spiral staircases and glass-enclosed elevators and in the middle stood a grand piano played by a man in a tuxedo. It was an elegant and costly experience.

The gourmet food floor was a wonderland. Wherever we travelled, Lennie would always buy coffee beans. At the *Samartine*, the beans were in glass jars with lids. The idea was to lift the lid and sniff it to see if you liked the scent. Apparently, Lennie couldn't get enough of a scent off the lid, so he stuck his nose in the jar. He *still* wasn't satisfied and dipped his hand in the jar, held the beans, and sniffed so hard I thought he would inhale the beans out of his hand. Then to my dismay, he returned the beans to the jar.

I stood there with my mouth open staring at him. "Whaaat?" he asked.

"I can't believe you just did that."

"Did what?" He saw nothing wrong with his behavior.

"I hope you are going to buy that coffee," I said, noting the look of horror frozen on the salesman's face.

When Lennie motioned that he wanted to buy the coffee, the man got a bag, a scoop, and tweezers, and began picking the individual beans off the top layer, while giving Lennie sidelong looks of disgust. He didn't use the scoop until he picked off the entire layer, one bean at a time.

We bought a few more items in the store, one of which was a large chocolate bar. Lennie, his hands full, set everything on the counter to get his credit card out. After the sale was rung up, the salesman offered to put all purchases into one large bag to make it easier to carry. He scooped everything into the shopping bag except the chocolate, which he deftly slid under the counter, winking at me. Lennie completed the transaction and pocketed his card. As we were walking away, he opened the shopping bag and looked in.

"Hey, where's my chocolate?"

The salesman was snickering, "I deedn't tink you would mees it, monsieur. Eet ees a teep, nes pas?" Who says Frenchmen have no sense of humor!

40.

Exit Strategy

Revenge can be sweet. On retiring from 16 years with two state agencies, I got my opportunity at the end of March 2003.

During the time I worked for the second agency, a new boss was politically appointed. "Oh, isn't she wonderful," fellow workers gushed, "so much nicer than the last boss." "We'll see," I said.

The new boss' smile was too wide to be genuine. She laughed often and loudly.

She interviewed all 17 employees to ask us what our jobs were so she could "get to know us." My co-workers thought it was great that she was taking the time with us. "We'll see," I said.

During my initial interview I explained that my career began as a consumer representative with the first state agency. I was promoted to supervisor. After taking a lateral transfer to the second agency, I was promoted to communications specialist. I wrote speeches for the boss and advised her on how to speak to the press. I developed and maintained good relations with television, radio and newspaper reporters, and issued press releases.

The boss never indicated that she was displeased with my work. Imagine my surprise when during a yearly evaluation she told me that I had to get more involved, be proactive. What did she want me to do? Make up the news? She didn't do anything newsworthy except attend meetings.

She joined every national or regional association based in Boston, which just happened to be her hometown, ensuring she had three or four monthly expense-paid visits.

Our agency belonged to a national association of consumer advocates. To become proactive as my boss ordered, I began communicating with the national director and my public relations counterparts in other states. We planned and developed a public relations committee to assist other consumer agencies with their local media relations. I was even elected chairman. We then organized seminars to be given at the annual conference in Washington, D.C.

I kept my boss informed of my activities with minutes of our bi-weekly phone meetings. I submitted my request to attend the conference, but two weeks before the big day, my boss informed me that I would not be attending. She was sending one of the attorneys. I knew that he was going to the conference just to schmooze and play golf. The national director even called my boss on my behalf, but she would not let me go. My teammates were highly disappointed. I spent hours on the phone with them and with the director who had to take over my role at the conference.

Subsequently, my boss received a letter from the national director attesting to the success of the seminars and my role in establishing them. My boss never mentioned the letter. Two weeks later, she sent me an email saying that the national office appreciated my efforts. She never mentioned it again. About two months later, my job was eliminated.

When I received the layoff notice, my boss was unaware that under union rules I had the right to take a lower paying position in lieu of the layoff. Which I did. She wasn't rid of me yet. She called me into her office and told me that one of the attorneys would be training me for my new position – entry level consumer assistant, *six pay grades lower*. My designated training attorney had no clue what a consumer assistant did. In fact, he avoided speaking to consumers. I reminded the boss that in my previous position I supervised 10 consumer assistants. I was sent back to my desk.

The next day, my inbox was full of public relations assignments. I stacked them neatly and deposited them on the training attorney's desk with a note. *This is not my job anymore. Since you seem to be the designated public relations person, good luck.*

During the next month, I was ignored. My duties were to answer infrequent consumer calls and to set up a website and keep it updated. Meanwhile, the boss decorated the office. She bought furniture and a dozen floor plants for the foyer. Those plants received more attention from her than I did. The boss strolled around the office checking on the plants, adding a little water here, trimming a leaf there. Weeks went by with no communication, even though she had to pass my cubicle every day on the way to her office.

When the state offered all employees a golden handshake, I decided to take it. I was old enough and had worked with the state long enough to qualify for an early retirement. I did not have to give notice to retire. I knew I would not be replaced. Every day I took something home with me – pictures of my family, awards and certificates I earned, my desk plants, chair cushion, until nothing personal was left.

On my last day, the boss was in Boston. Perfect. I put my retirement notice in her inbox. Then I took one of the floor plants and placed it in my chair with a nametag: *Judy's replacement*. I left the building.

One of the secretaries later told me what happened after I left. When the boss returned from Boston, she noticed that one plant was missing. She flew around the room in a rage looking for it, accusing the cleaning crew of taking it, blaming the secretary for not knowing what happened. She contacted the two other agencies in the building to see if they knew anything. She brought the cleaning crew in for questioning. She had security search the building. Meanwhile, she never asked where I was, nor did she check my cubicle, though she flew by it many times. She spent the entire day questioning people.

Finally, someone suggested she check my cubicle. When the boss saw the plant with its nametag sitting in my chair, she turned purple, yelling, "Get that out of there!" She hurried to her office and slammed her door. The rest of the staff had a good laugh.

Two years later, I was called for jury duty at the courthouse across the square from the building where I'd worked. I hadn't been back since I retired but I was meeting a friend for lunch. As I crossed the square, I noticed a small group of people that I didn't know standing in front of the building smoking. "That's her," one of them said. "That's the plant lady." They all laughed and congratulated me. My exit into retirement was talked about for years.

41.

Overwhelming Sadness

Besides retiring in 2003, I survived another life changing event. Lennie died.

He had been diagnosed with pancreatic cancer in October of 2002. Back then, the diagnosis was death within three months. Lennie signed up for a double-blind drug trial which bought him a year. He took the drug every day but also had chemotherapy once a week. He did not lose his hair or his appetite. The only side effect he had was extreme tiredness two days after the chemo treatment. He still bowled with his team. We still travelled. Everything seemed normal.

Lennie's ankles began to swell and the doctor put him on a diuretic. Then his blood pressure dropped. For a week, he yo-yoed between swollen ankles with no diuretic and low blood pressure with the diuretic.

He was admitted to the hospital on Friday and spent the weekend undergoing tests. His blood pressure was low, and he was having trouble breathing. I kept trying to help him breathe. I would have breathed for him if I could have. On Monday night, he told me to go home and get some rest. As I was leaving, he reminded me to bring his clothes in the morning because he was determined to come home, against medical advice. Then, unexpectedly, he said in a small voice, "I'm scared." I made some joke about him being a big man and he was the one who scared others. I guess deep down I really knew that he wouldn't be coming home.

Early the next morning, the phone woke me. A nurse told me Lennie died in his sleep at 4 a.m. on Tuesday, September 16, 2003. Although he had pancreatic cancer, he died of heart failure. I believe that Lennie sent me home from the hospital to spare me the final hours of his struggle.

I spoke with his doctor who told me that the tests showed there was no cancer left. In my heart I know the chemo killed him. If the doctor had stopped the chemo when the cancer disappeared, Lennie may have lived longer.

It has been 18 years and the treatment for pancreatic cancer hasn't changed with the drug Lennie took and chemotherapy. Life expectancy hasn't increased much.

Lennie and I had such a short time together and they were the happiest years of my life.

42.

Letters to My Dead Husband
– excerpts

November 15, 2003
Dearest Lennie,

   It's been two months since you died. I expected to be arguing with you the next day about whether you should come home against medical advice. I did not expect that you would not be coming home. You often told me that if I died when I had my heart attack, you would have been pissed at me. Boy, am I pissed at you! I'm also pissed at myself for not recognizing the signs and staying with you overnight at the hospital.

   When you said you were scared, I wanted to tell you that there was nothing to fear. But you didn't want to listen to my near-death experience. I feel awful that I went home to get some sleep instead of staying with you. The doctor said there was nothing I could have done. You were asleep when your heart stopped. I wasn't prepared to lose you so soon. I believed you were having a temporary setback – that as soon as your medicines were rebalanced, you would be OK again. Damn!

Thanksgiving, 2003
Dear Lennie,

   I remember a dream I had one night when I fell asleep with my head on your shoulder. I dreamt I woke up next to Christina. It came true. Maureen and her family came for Thanksgiving. She and her husband slept downstairs. The boys stayed in the guest room. Christina slept with me.

December 14, 2003
My Dearest Lennie,

It's December already. You've been gone three months. I'm no longer crying my eyes out every day but I'm not sleeping well. The plumber started working on the bathroom today. I decided to go ahead with the renovations we planned since the money was set aside. You'd like the separate shower stall.

I'm still mad at you for dying and I wish you were here. I talk to you all the time while watching TV. I pretend you're sitting in your recliner – there is still a faint scent of you in the chair. Sometimes I sniff it or your shirts I kept in the closet. I hope you knew how very much I loved you. The years we had together were the happiest of my life. My only regret is that we had such a short time together. I love you every day.

September 15-16, 2004
Lennie My Dear,

A year has passed. I can't believe it. Sometimes I feel like our whole relationship was only a dream. You had more influence on me than you ever knew. Perhaps you know now. I loved you with all my heart and I know how much you loved me. I lit the Yahrzeit candle in the evening of the 15th and it burned for 24 hours. I went to the cemetery and sprinkled Dunkin' Donuts coffee on your grave in lieu of flowers. You liked coffee more than anything. Sorry if I got some on your feet – I poured it at both ends.

May 30, 2005
Dearest Lennie,

I had intentions of writing on the eve of our anniversary but got bogged down by the computer. Happy anniversary, my love, wherever you are. I hope you know how much I love and miss you. I'm going to a family picnic for Memorial Day. I doubt anyone will mention our anniversary but that's OK – I remember. It would have been our eighth anniversary. I had hoped for more, but I treasure every year we shared. Your brother told me that before we met, you were an unhappy, angry person. He thinks you died happy because of our time together. I hope that's true. Good night, my love.

June 23, 2005
My Dearest Lennie,

You have left me for good this time. I don't feel your presence in the house anymore. I hope that means you've moved on to a better place.

You didn't believe in "that stuff" – ghosts, out of body experiences, premonitions. Yet, here you were, making house calls on me after you died.

You were such a Yankees fan. That trick you did when the Red Sox won the World Series was sensational – exploding the kitchen light and the bulb in the living room lamp the moment they won. You always said the Sox wouldn't win against the Yankees as long as you were alive. By the way, I didn't appreciate having to clean up all that glass.

I know the exact moment you left the house. It was the night of the summer solstice, June 21. I was in bed. When I looked through the doorway, I saw your essence – ghost, spirit, aura – standing by the washer like you always did when getting ready for bed. You would put your clothes in the laundry basket and shake your booty at me.

I saw you clearly. You waved at me. You must have known that it was alright to move on – that I would be OK. I am OK. I'm also very sad. I miss you more now. The house feels empty.

Good-bye, my love. Until we meet again.
Your beloved and loving wife,
Judy

Part V

Alone Again

43.

No Customer Service

After Lennie died, I put our joint accounts in my name only, except for our cell phone. I went to the *Sprint* store and explained that my husband had died, and I wanted the account to be put in my name. I was told that I had to contact the company by computer. What if I don't have one, I asked. The rep merely shrugged his shoulder. You would think that if you have a problem with your phone, you could resolve it by phone.

I wrote on my computer:

Dear Sprint Customer Service,

My husband, Leonard Slitt, is deceased. I would like our account to be put into my name only. The account number is xxx and the billing address is xxx. Since my husband signed up for the phone originally, I am secondary on the account so I cannot make changes. Please let me know what paperwork I need to do.

Sincerely,

Judith Humphrey, widow of Leonard Slitt.

The reply came a week later:

Dear Mr. Slitt,

We received your request to change your account. You will have to come to one of our Sprint stores in person to make any changes to your account.

Sincerely, Customer Service Rep

How aggravating! I wrote back:

Dear Customer Service Rep,

What part of deceased do you not understand? Deceased as in dead as a doornail, as in gone from this life, as in six feet under. Do you want me to dig him up and bring him to the store so you can see for yourself?

If this request is not resolved by the end of this month, I will have to cancel the account.

Sincerely,

Judith Humphrey, still the WIDOW of Leonard Slitt

The reply:

Dear Mrs. Humphrey,

I apologize for the mix-up, but you will still have to come into the store to resolve your problem. Bring a copy of the death certificate and we will begin to set you up as a new customer with your own account.

Sincerely,

Supervisor

This was not what I wanted. As a new customer, I would have to establish a credit history when I already had a five-year credit history with *Sprint*. The contract ran out a few months later. During that time, I had no access to it. The company continued to accept my monthly check. I cancelled the account, switched to *Verizon* and have been phoning happily ever after with a senior citizen discount.

44.

Volunteering

I wanted to give back to the hospital for all the care Lennie received during his year battling pancreatic cancer. I signed up to volunteer.

My first job was assembling the medical charts of patients getting outpatient surgery. Having directed volunteers in assembly-line projects – like folding paperwork and stuffing envelopes – I tend to arrange materials logically so that the task can be accomplished in the minimum amount of time. I quickly learned that when it comes to older volunteers, efficiency is frowned upon. When I turned a three-day job into a three-hour job, I was told to put the materials back into their chaotic arrangement because the other volunteers didn't like change. The underlying story was that they enjoyed the three days a week it took them to finish the job. They could get free lunch on those days and it gave them something to do.

I asked for a different job. I was assigned to push a cart loaded with free things – magazines, reading glasses, chapsticks, videos, books – to patients' rooms. Patients could keep everything but the videos. I visited briefly with each of the people. For anyone celebrating a birthday, I brought flowers and cake and even sang *Happy Birthday*. I always wore a smile and a funny hat to cheer them up.

One day, I met two doctors in the elevator. I was wearing antlers. The doctors giggled. I told them, "It's your job to make the patients well. It's my job to make them smile."

The final hospital volunteer job I took was a 'cuddler.' I took care of babies who were born hooked on drugs. I rocked them, sang to them, fed and burped them. Besides the addiction, they suffered from a variety of physical ailments, from heart to digestive problems. While being weaned off the drugs, they were in considerable pain and cried a lot. My singing calmed them. It took three to four months to get them totally off the drugs.

While cuddlers were tending the babies, the addicted mothers attended group therapy sessions to get themselves off drugs. One of the mothers was a military wife whose husband was in Afghanistan. She would wait till I arrived so she could talk to me before she left for therapy.

A year and a half later, I was called to take care of a baby in the Neonatal Intensive Care Unit. The mother requested me. She was the military wife whose baby girl I rocked through withdrawal. At first, I thought she gave birth to another addicted baby. When she came to the NICU, she was proud to tell me that not only did she kick her drug habit, but she was enrolled in nursing school. Her husband had come back home, and her first baby was strong and healthy. The second little girl was born with heart problems not caused by addiction. She told me that I had taken such good care of her first born that she wanted me to care for her second baby as well.

I volunteered for 11 years until the hospital was taken over by a big corporation. The new company eliminated all the volunteer positions. I often wonder about those babies – if anyone rocked or sang to them.

The day of my interview to be a volunteer usher at the Bushnell Theater, I wore a Monty Python T-shirt that proclaimed, *I'm not dead yet.* I bought it at the theater when I saw the show two weeks before my interview. It worked – I got to join the 700 volunteers who were part of the Bushnell family.

The perks of being a Bushnell volunteer were that you got to see the shows for free and you got a free non-alcoholic beverage during intermission. The drawback was that you had to be able to stand for five hours. Volunteers were only allowed to sit in the last row of the balcony and only when no patrons were seated there. That hardly ever happened.

The actual work took about two of the five hours. Only a half hour of that time was spent ushering patrons to their seats. The rest of the time we guarded the emergency exits, stuffed programs with fliers announcing cast changes, collected tickets, guarded the props, handed out programs, and gave directions. The most asked question was, "Where is the restroom?"

It was exciting volunteering at the theater and getting to see shows like *The Lion King*, *Les Misérables*, and *The Phantom of the Opera*. My only contact with a celebrity came the night of the *Peter, Paul and Mary* concert. I was standing in the back of the orchestra section near the sound equipment. Peter Yarrow ran from the stage, tripped, lost his balance and fell into me. I was leaning against the wall, so I was able to catch him. He said, "Excuse me, excuse me, excuse me," bowed and went to speak to the sound engineer. A brush with celebrity!

I attended a newcomers meeting at the Plainville Senior Center. The director explained the programs and activities that were available. She added that if anyone had a skill they'd like to teach, to speak with her after the meeting.

I had taken photography classes in college and my photographs had been published in magazines and newspapers. Most of my published work was done as part of my public relations positions. However, I did wedding photography as a side job.

This photo published in the Hartford Courant *prompted me to teach photography at the Senior Center and establish the Snappy Seniors Camera Club*

I offered to teach a class in photo composition. My goal was to teach people how to take clear pictures of their grandchildren, pets or trips without a distracting background.

Nine seniors signed up for the first class. I taught four sessions. The first was instruction and demonstration of the elements of a good photo. The other three classes were field trips to practice photography.

I taught the class five times to a total of 40 students. I formed a camera club, the Snappy Seniors, which had 30 active members. Club activities included photo excursions, displays in local libraries and nursing homes, and honing photography skills through video lectures and practice. Members showed and discussed their work at monthly meetings.

The members were aged from 60s to 90s. We lost six of the original members but added a few new ones over the years.

One of the members won a photo contest that I had also entered. She was afraid to tell me that she'd won – she thought I'd be mad at her. On the contrary, I was so happy for her – she had never won a contest before. And I was happy that I had played a small part in her success.

45.

The Solo

I am a musician. Music has always been part of my life. Besides piano, I also took violin lessons for six years and voice lessons for two. Somewhere along the way, I decided it was more fun and less work to sing with instead of accompanying a chorus. I sight-read music and have a decent soprano voice. Most of the choruses I joined were by audition only and I had performed with symphony orchestras. I also directed a choir in an Air Force Chapel, and was a cantor for ten years in my parish church.

The first chorus I joined in Connecticut was based at the University of Hartford's Hartt College. It was composed of young music majors and people from the community. The blend of young and seasoned voices gave the chorus a bright and rich tone.

The standard concert dress for choral members is a long-sleeved white blouse and floor-length black skirt for the women, and a black tuxedo for the men. I had purchased my long black skirt when I sang with my first formal chorus in the 70s. I replaced the blouse several times over the years but the skirt never went out of style. It didn't wear out because I only wore it twice a year for winter and spring concerts and I never sat down in it. I realized how long I had been singing when I was waiting in line to take the stage in Hartford. The young girls behind me were discussing their skirts, where they bought them, the material and the cost. After the concert, the director approached me and asked, "Is something wrong?"

"No, why do you ask?"

"Well, just before we went onstage you looked pale," he said.

"Oh that must have been when I realized that my skirt is older than half the chorus members."

The last chorus I sang with was in Bristol. It was a typical community chorus; no auditions. Anyone could sign up. The accompanist, a former director of the chorus, invited people to form three smaller groups to work on special pieces for the Christmas concert. At the first rehearsal she held auditions for a solo part, and although I was a new member, I tried out. Since I had never auditioned for a solo before, I was very nervous. I got the part and spent the next week learning it.

At the following rehearsal, favoritism reared its ugly head. The accompanist called me aside on my way in and said through a tight little smile, "Oh, Judy, one of the other women wasn't here last week to audition and she really wants to do the solo. Would you mind sharing the solo with her?"

"Yes," I said. Just as she started to smile thinking that I had agreed I added, "I would mind very much. I auditioned for the solo and I got it. It wouldn't be fair to take it away from me now."

Of course, there would be trouble from then on because the other woman was one of the accompanist's friends. From that moment, she did everything in her power to discourage my performance. She claimed I wasn't singing loud enough, and repeatedly shushed the chorus in the background. She tried to humiliate me by making me sing the part without any accompaniment, hoping I would sing off-key. She didn't know that I have the gift of relative pitch. It's not perfect pitch but better than most. She also didn't cue in my part but I came in on time anyway.

Finally, the night of the concert arrived. When I saw the program, I wasn't surprised that my name wasn't in it. Soloists with the other groups were given microphones. I was not. I knew that the concert was being filmed but when my first solo line came up, the camera wasn't anywhere near me. OK, think, how do I get noticed? I sang my heart out on the second line while the camera slowly panned toward me, but I was finished singing before it got to me. By the third time I was determined to call attention to myself so I took a small step forward and gestured toward the sky because the lyrics were something about angels descending from above. The accompanist, who had not even acknowledged my existence up to this point, gave me a look dirty enough to wither a bouquet of flowers. I beamed as I stepped back into place.

After the performance, I managed a quick little curtsy toward where my friends and family were seated, then hustled off the stage. My fellow singers congratulated me. From that day forward if the accompanist saw me heading in her direction, she'd turn and walk away. If she happened upon me head on, she'd look right through me. I'd smile and say loudly, "Hello. How are you this evening?"

I love to sing and I'm good at it, but I knew I would never again sing for her or any organization she was connected to. I still have the DVD of the night I sang a solo and my spirit soared in triumph.

46.

Tangle with the TSA

I travel by air about twice a year, for pleasure and because some of my children and grandchildren live clear across the country. Shortly before my 70th birthday, I flew to Hawaii to visit my granddaughter and her first baby, a son born in Honolulu. I had been to Hawaii on vacation more than 40 years ago. Things had changed – a lot. Though I had flown many places in the interim, I compared my first flight to Hawaii with this one.

In 1975, the stewardesses – all women – were also nurses. They dressed in uniforms with high heels, nylons, hats and gloves. In 2012, flight attendants were men and women. Most of them wore Bermuda shorts or khaki pants and sneakers.

Passengers used to dress in their Sunday best because flying, which was expensive, was reserved for special occasions. White linen cloths were attached to the headrests so you wouldn't have to rest your head in someone else's dandruff. They were changed after every flight. Passengers were given a pillow, a blanket, free hot meals, drinks and snacks, and a choice of magazines to read. Everyone was polite and 'the friendly skies' really were friendly.

Now we practically undress to get through security, emptying our pockets and removing our shoes, even flip-flops. My travel agent informed me that 70-year-olds do not have to remove their shoes. I thought that was great. I would be 70 in two weeks, so I confidently marched through security with my shoes on.

The TSA stopped me. "How old are you?" he asked.

"I'll be 70 in two weeks," I replied. "Is that close enough?"

He looked at me sideways. "Take your shoes off," he said without smiling.

"But I thought that you could leave your shoes on at 70 years old."

"Take your shoes off," he repeated.

"C'mon, aren't I close enough to 70?"

"It's 75. Take your shoes off."

"Seriously?" But he still wasn't smiling. "OK," I said, " I'm 75."

"No, you're not. You just told me you're 69."

"I lied."

"Take your shoes off."

The man behind me stepped up, looked the agent in the eye and said, "I'm 75." He got to keep his shoes on. When we got through the line, the man said to me, "Hell, if I knew that, I would have said I was 75 five years ago."

I also try to avoid checking luggage now because there is no guarantee that you'll see it again. I left for Hawaii with a carry-on and a camera case. My carry-on was efficiently packed with enough clothes and supplies for 3 weeks in Hawaii. Everything had a place. Of course, the TSA just had to rifle through my belongings. Honestly, do I look like a terrorist? Must have been the shoe conversation.

My carefully packed bag was torn apart looking for – what, I don't know. The agent finally held up a rubber-tipped dental pick. "What's this?" he asked.

"It's a dental pick."

"I have to take it."

"Why?"

"It has a point on it."

"It's a rubber tip."

"You can go back to the counter and have it shipped home, or I can toss it."

"You've got to be kidding."

"We don't kid," he said. "Ship it or toss it?"

"Toss it," I said defeated.

I stepped to the side to repack my bag on the floor. Good thing the agent didn't hear me mutter, "Are you afraid I will give someone terminal gingivitis?" Really!

47.

My Heart Goes On — 2008

"Anyone would get winded walking around the Colosseum in Rome," I told my cardiologist. "I also climbed the Spanish Steps and the 101 stairs to enter the Church of St. Peter in Chains. On the trip home, I had to lug my suitcase and jog a mile between gates at Madrid's airport to make the connecting flight."

"None of that explains the numbness in your left hand," he said. "Your stress test was fine, but it doesn't show everything that's going on. I'm sending you for an angiogram just to be sure."

My sister drove me to the hospital for the test. It was supposed to take about two hours after which we were going to lunch. I was kept awake during the angiogram. A catheter was inserted through the main artery in my groin.

When I'd had my previous angiogram, I'd watched the procedure on a monitor. It was fascinating, and I hadn't felt anything. This time, that same doctor blocked my view. I was about to protest when I felt a pain in my chest.

"Hey," I complained, "that hurts."

"Be quiet," he said.

The pain persisted. I screamed, "I said stop that. You're hurting me."

"Be quiet. Be quiet," he said. "I'm working on it."

"Please stop it. That really hurts."

In the waiting room at 10:30 when I was due out of the procedure, the nurse sat down next to my sister and took her hand.

"Oh, crap. This can't be good," my sister said.

"There's been a complication," the nurse said. "Everything's going to be OK. It will just take longer than expected." Then she left my sister alone in the waiting room for two more hours. The nurse didn't give her any more information.

When I opened my eyes and saw my sister, she was pale and had been crying. It was afternoon. "What happened," I asked. The nurse told me the doctor would be in to speak with me shortly.

"Good," I said. "My sister and I are late for lunch."

"You're not going anywhere for a few days."

While getting settled in Intensive Care, I could see my sister leaning against the wall. She's fair skinned like I am. Her complexion seemed to be blending in with the wall color – pale green. I watched her slowly slide down the wall until she was sitting on the floor. She's diabetic and hadn't eaten since breakfast.

"Get her some food," I said, "or she'll end up in bed with me."

Finally, the doctor came in and explained. During the angiogram, he'd found a blocked artery and had inserted a stent to open it up. However, my heart had grown a new artery around the blockage in an area that was hidden from the camera. I began experiencing pain because the stent blocked the new artery. It fought back, trying to eject the foreign object.

Although not common, the human heart can heal itself with the proper encouragement: medication, diet and exercise.

The doctor looked at me with tears in his eyes and said, "I am so sorry you had to go through this. I should have seen that extra artery. I am deeply sorry."

"Doctor, you are not God. Everything happens for a reason. Thank you for doing your best. I'm still here."

48.

Christmases Past

December 2016 – It's time for the obligatory annual Christmas letters to come pouring in. I separate them into two categories. The *my life is worse than yours, oh how I suffer* category is a real bummer. But most of the missives fit into the *everything is rosy and wonderful fa-la-la* category. No one's real life is that perfect. You mean that you never had a child eat too much Christmas candy, puke all over his room, then calmly direct you in the cleaning process from his perch on the top bunk bed? "Mom, you missed a spot over there."

Or that you never had your daughter come home from school on the last day before Christmas vacation with bloody palms.

"Why are you holding your hands behind your back? Let me see them."

"You don't want to see them."

"Yes, I do, my little gymnast, show me. Eewwww!"

"I told you that you wouldn't want to see them."

My rosy friends write letters that sound like fairy tales to me. *We took four trips across the pond this year and spent a month in the Netherlands enjoying the tulip festival. Our daughter received her MD this spring and is working at* Johns Hopkins *and our attorney son was promoted to partner at his law firm in New York fa-la-la.* My letter the same year, if I could have afforded postage, would have said, *I was fired on Christmas Eve and now I do my grocery shopping in my mother's freezer tra-la.*

The friends in the *my life is worse than yours* category usually think that telling folks about their operations, or details about every illness they've suffered, is somehow entertaining to the general populace. Here's a news flash – it's not the slightest bit amusing. Personally, I have written a few letters in each category over the years. I apologize, although some had to be written – such as, I got married, I lost my job, my husband died – the events that make up a life.

A few Christmases stand out in my mind and for better or worse, have shaped my attitude towards the holiday.

My earliest memory of Christmas was in 1950. I asked Santa Claus for a 'chain drive' three-wheeler. It had brakes like a bicycle. I had been wanting one for a couple of years, but my parents kept telling me I wasn't old enough. Finally, Christmas day arrived. I ran to the living room and couldn't believe my eyes. There, in front of the Christmas tree was not one, but two red chain drives with red bows on them – one for me and one for my sister who was two years younger. I burst into tears.

In 1957 as a teenager, I earned enough money babysitting and teaching piano lessons to buy gifts for my parents for Christmas. I bought my mother a warm robe. It was white and fluffy with red velvet trim. She loved red. I beamed when she gave me a big hug and thanked me. A couple of weeks later, on a chilly morning, I asked her why she wasn't wearing her robe. She said, "Oh, Sister Marie at the convent was sick and she needed something warm to wear so I gave it to her." My heart broke. After that, I gave my mother Mass cards for gifts. At least she couldn't give those away. To this day, I cherish any gifts I get from my children and grandchildren, especially hand-made ones. I still have my son's gift to me he made in first grade – a piece of cloth decorated with pasta. I also kept a shelf my daughter made in shop class.

In 1963, Ed and I spent our first Christmas season as a married couple driving from Mississippi home to Connecticut. We had no money. Of course, the family bought us Christmas gifts, except our parents who fortunately gave us cash. On Christmas morning, we went out to the only store that was open – the drug store, and bought little gifts for everyone. We still had no money.

The following Christmas we were living in Tripoli, Libya. We had no telephones or communications of any kind. Ed arrived home on Christmas Eve from a two-and-a-half-month mission and I was very happy to see him. He was exhausted, in a foul mood and went directly to bed. I rocked my baby and sang to him until he fell asleep. Ed bought me a model train set which I still have.

We returned from Libya in January 1967. Although it was after the holidays, our families had delayed their Christmas celebrations until we returned.

My most memorable and joyous Christmas was in 1996. My boyfriend of six months, Lennie, had moved in with me in September. Since he was Jewish and I was Catholic, we celebrated both Hanukkah and Christmas. We gave each other little gifts each night of Hanukkah, and on Christmas Eve, I went to midnight Mass. It was a very warm December that year and when I got home, I noticed that two of the pansies in my flower bed were blooming. We opened our Christmas gifts and emptied our stockings. But apparently, I didn't completely empty mine. Something was stuck in the toe. It was a small box. I opened it and found a diamond ring.

"I don't know what to say," I said.

Lennie said, "Say yes."

"Yes."

We were married five months later.

49.

I'm Not Done Yet

February 23, 2020. As with the other two heart attacks, I didn't see this one coming. It was a typical Sunday night; I was watching TV in my nightgown. Suddenly, I felt I was going to be sick to my stomach. The last time that had happened was over a decade before. I had heard on the news that there was a new flu going around, but I'd had my flu shot.

Coming out of the bathroom, I felt faint and lay down on the floor. Another wave of nausea hit me; I felt terrible. I was wearing my I've-fallen-and-I-can't-get-up monitor, and so I pushed the button. A voice said, "Hello, this is James. How can I help you?"

I described how I felt. James kept me talking while he called for help. The police arrived in less than a minute, followed by the ambulance. Unlike my first ambulance ride, when asked where I wanted to go, I didn't say Disney World. I just said New Britain – it's the nearest hospital. The paramedics wrapped me in a blanket and rolled me out to the ambulance. I had no coat, no shoes, and it was February.

In the emergency room, I was still sick to my stomach. The doctor thought I had the flu or food poisoning, until my blood test came back from the lab. "Oh, honey," he said. "You don't have the flu; you're having a heart attack."

I couldn't believe it. I had no symptoms of a heart attack. The doctor said they were getting another ambulance to send me to Hartford. "I'd rather stay here," I said. "You don't have a choice," he said. Hartford Hospital is larger and better equipped to handle heart problems.

The trip didn't take long – it was 11:30 p.m. – and I was taken directly to surgery. Four hours later I was in the ICU with a band aid on my wrist, having had four stents placed in my arteries. By 8 a.m., I was sitting up eating breakfast. I felt like a medical miracle.

When my dad was 75, he had open heart surgery to replace four blocked arteries. He survived the operation but only lived for a short time after. For the first two days following his surgery, he was unconscious and hooked up to machines. He kept having strokes because he was off blood thinners. First, he lost his speech, then all his movements. Within a month he was gone. Medicine has come a long way since then.

I was not allowed to drive for six weeks and then by the time I could drive, the world was in lockdown due to the Covid 19 pandemic, so there was no place to go. It was nightmarish. Businesses were closed, streets were abandoned, people stayed in their homes. And the country was out of toilet paper. I couldn't figure that out because the symptoms were high fever and respiratory problems.

Shopping was either online or by phone. Delivery trucks proliferated. Most people wore masks and washed their hands often. Schools were closed. Kids were home, glued to their cell phones or the TV until distance learning began.

I learned from the other two heart attacks that the only way to get back to living was through cardiac rehab. Because of the pandemic, the hospital wasn't open for classes until June. I attended three days a week during the summer. It was the only time I left my house.

My computer and I became intimately involved. I had Alexa to talk to. I watched movies on TV. I read books. I trolled the internet. Finally, I began writing.

I had recently reconnected with an acquaintance from 30 years ago, Phil Blumenkrantz. He is a retired newspaper reporter and a former editor. I sent him the first chapter of my story to get his opinion. He encouraged me to continue writing. He volunteered to edit it for me. Thus began a two-year long adventure that kept us both busy during the pandemic.

When people ask me what I did during the pandemic, I tell them I had a heart attack. Then I wrote this book.

Epilogue

The thought of writing a book has always appealed to me. Not because I'm famous or rich, but because of friends asking me what it had been like being a military wife, moving around while raising children. I've told them stories of places I've lived. I injected a sense of humor despite the difficulties I encountered.

My friends told me that I really ought to write a book. I dismissed the idea because who would want to read it.

While the idea kept resurfacing, I kept finding excuses for not writing. Until the pandemic hit. I would be stuck alone at home for an unknown period so – why not?

This is my story, as I lived it, as I remember it. I am sure Mike and Maureen remember it differently. I am sure Ed remembers it differently. But this is my story, my feelings. I believe we learn from life's challenges.

The greatest thing you'll ever learn
is just to love and be loved in return.

Nature Boy, Nat King Cole.

Acknowledgements

I am grateful to the Wrogue Writers, Erv Dworkin, Rob Koekkoek, Margaret Lemasurier, Paul Macca, Sue Theriault, and Elaine Wyzka who, over the course of two years, listened to and commented on my beginning writings and revisions.

Special thanks to Phil Blumenkrantz for driving me to complete this book during the pandemic. I will never forget you.

Sue Fitzmaurice, writer, editor and publisher at Rebel Magic Books, has made it possible for me to fulfill my dream of becoming a published author. Thank you so much.

REBEL
MAGIC
BOOKS

www.rebelmagicbooks.com

Made in United States
North Haven, CT
20 February 2022

16311646R00104